The Guinness Book of Me

A Memoir of Record

Steven Church

simon & schuster
New York   London
Toronto   Sydney

SIMON & SCHUSTER
Rockefeller Center
1230 Avenue of the Americas
New York, NY 10020

For information about special discounts for bulk purchases,
please contact Simon & Schuster Special Sales:
1-800-456-6798 or business@simonandschuster.com

Designed by Jeanette Olender
Manufactured in the United States of America

10 9 8 7 6 5 4 3 2 1

Library of Congress Cataloging-in-Publication Data
Church, Steven.
The Guinness book of me : a memoir of record / Steven Church
p. cm.
1. Church, Steven—Childhood and youth. 2. Boys—Kansas—Biography.
3. Brothers—Kansas—Biography. 4. Risk-taking (Psychology) in adolescence—Kansas.
5. Kansas—Biography. 6. Guinness book of records (New York, N.Y.) I. Title.
CT275.A1C48   2005
818'.609—dc22   [B]   2004056578

ISBN 0-7432-6695-1

For fathers, sons, and brothers—
especially my own

Records.

Author's Note.   xi

S.T.E.V.E.N. A Personal Index.   1
Boy, Misfit.   4
Bond, Closest.   14
Smashing, Bare Hand.   24
Commitment, Longest.   34
Boy, Bionic.   40
Tongues, Speaking In.   52
Knives, Sharpest.   60
Diet, Strangest.   72
Guns, Youngest.   78
Danger Boys, World's Greatest.   90
Well, Biggest.   132
Skin, Toughest.   144
Trenchermen, World's Greatest.   148
Joints, Weakest.   158
Hero, Home Run.   176
Scars, Most, on Right Side of Body.   182
Fall, Hardest.   200
Transportation, Most Dangerous.   204
Escape, Greatest.   220

Acknowledgments, Most Deserving Of.   223

Author's Note.

This book uses quotations and references taken from the Giant 1980 Super-Edition of the *Guinness Book of World Records,* edited by Norris McWhirter (and a few pieces from a 1982 edition). It is quite possible and even likely that many records I reference have been surpassed and replaced with even greater (or lesser) achievements in their respective categories. I rely on outdated reference books because these are the very same books I owned as a child, and that seems like a good enough reason.

This book is a work of creative nonfiction. Many (but not all) names have been changed. Other things have been added or subtracted, highlighted, distorted, possibly corrupted, compressed, expanded, exaggerated, or dramatized for emotional effect, and I promise that the reasons for this are very convincing. This book is full of detailed speculation. Any resemblance between reality and my imagination is purely coincidental and unintentional. This is not a book of fact. This is a story.

S. T. E. V. E. N.

A Personal Index*

S. See-Saw. Sermon. Shaving. Sheaf Tossing. Shoe Shining. Shorthand, Fastest. Showering. Singing. Skateboarding. Slinging. Smoke-Ring Blowing. Snowshoe Travel. Speech-Listening. Spinning. Spitting. Stair-Climbing. Standing Up. Stilt Walking. Stowaway. Stretcher Bearing. String Ball, Largest. Submergence. Suggestion Box. Swinging.

T. Tailoring. Talking. Pulling with Teeth. Tightrope. Tire Stacking. Treasure Finding. Tree Climbing. Tree Sitting. Typing, Fastest. Typing, Slowest. Typing, Longest.

E. Egg and Spoon Racing. Egg Drop. Egg-Shelling. Egg Throwing. Escapology.

V. Vacuum, Highest. Valve, Largest. Vase, Most Expensive. Vat. Vault. Vehicle, First Moon. Vein, Largest Human. Velocity. Venom. Verbs. Versatile Athlete. Verse, Longest Bible. Vertebrates. Viaduct. Village, Oldest. Vine.

☞ These are entries culled from the index to the 1980 Super-Edition of the *Guinness Book of World Records*.

1

Vineyard. Vintage, Oldest Wine. Violin. Violinist, Underwater. Virus. Viscosity. Visibility. Visible Object. Volcanoes. Vole. Volleyball. Voltages, Highest Shock. Voyage. Vulture, Slowest Wing Beat.

E. Eating Records: Baked Beans. Bananas. Beer. Bicycle. Champagne. Cheese. Chicken. Clams. Doughnuts. Eels. Eggs. Frankfurters. Gherkins. Grapes. Hamburgers. Ice Cream. Lemons. Meat. Milk. Oysters. Pancakes. Peanuts. Pickled Onions. Potato Chips. Potatoes. Prunes. Ravioli. Sandwiches. Sausages. Shellfish. Shrimps. Snails. Spaghetti. Tortillas.

N. Nails, Longest Finger. Names. Narcotics. National Anthems. National Debt. Natural Gas, see Gas. Naturist Resort. Navy, Largest. Necks, Longest Human. Needle Threading. Neon Sign. Nerve Gas. Nests. Newspapers. Newt, Largest. Night Club. Nile. Nonuplets. Noodle Making. Northern Lights. North Pole. Novelist, Most Prolific. Nuclear Arsenal. Nudist Camp. Nuggets. Number. Numeration. Nut. Nylon, Sheerest.

Most Variable Stature.

Adam Rainer, born in 1899 in Graz, Austria, measured 3 feet 10.45 inches at the age of 21. But then he suddenly started growing upwards at a rapid rate, and by 1931 he had reached 7 feet 1 3/4 inches. He became so weak as a result that he was bedridden for the rest of his life. He died on March 4, 1950, aged 51. (1980, 19)

Boy, Misfit.

The day the Book Fair came to school was charged with a static buzz of anticipation. I stood in the brick hallway of Hillcrest Elementary with the rest of my class, all of us bouncing around on our feet, chirping and twittering like finches at a feeder, waiting impatiently to be ushered into the room with the books.

I fingered the folded-up cash in my pocket and imagined the fantastical scene that awaited me—long tables piled high with colorful books of all shapes and sizes, all different authors and heroes—but always, *always* with my mind on the prize, the *Guinness Book of World Records*.

The tension was almost too much to take.

I stood there, shuffling around, and watched anxiously as the class ahead of mine filed out, their arms piled high with books, and I counted copies and made mental notes to see which titles were going fast. Dad had told my little brother Matt and me to "buy any book you want." But I already knew what book I wanted. There was no question about that. I wanted the latest edition of the *Guinness Book of World Records*. No, I *needed* it.

They set the books up on the stage in the gym, under the lights, and they'd pulled the big curtains closed so we were surrounded with purple velvet baffling, and I felt like I was visiting some kind of sacred purple space. Inside the curtains, it smelled like new books—that clean paper, cloth, and glue smell—combined with musty cardboard, and the heady lilac perfume on the soft-skinned PTO ladies who worked the Book Fair.

When my class finally got its turn, we had to move around the book tables in an orderly, single-file fashion, patiently examining the different genres, subjects, and titles. I hated waiting in line. The hot stage lights burned overhead and I felt little beads of sweat rising from my forehead. I impatiently lingered over the biographies of presidents and sports heroes, keeping an eye on my goal.

The Guinness Books glowed yellow and bright, almost lurid under the stage lights. It nearly killed me to watch the other children pawing at *my* books. I was gripped with the fear that by the time I got around the table, past all the Encyclopedia Brown and Judy Blume, past the Hardy Boys and Laura Ingalls Wilder, the Guinness Books would be gone. My heart began to race. I twisted my fingers into knots. Inside I was screaming, "Move!" while on the outside I squirmed and fidgeted, waiting my turn like a good boy. After much angst and sweat and internal screaming, I finally reached the books and clutched a copy to my chest, sniffing up the new-book aroma.

I'm convinced that they were just moments away from having to scrape me off the stage and call Dad at work to come get me. But I tend to exaggerate these sorts of things. I'm sure there was a box or two of the books under the table and, as soon as the table emptied, a new pile would appear. In any case I wasn't prepared to take that risk.

I couldn't bear the thought of missing a new edition. There wasn't much difference from one year to the next. Maybe a few new records or stats. Maybe a few new pictures. But that was enough for me. After school, when Matt was playing Atari or riding his bike in the yard, I'd disappear into my basement bedroom, pop in a cassette of the J. Geils Band or maybe some Styx, and study the book as if it was a sacred tome written on ancient parchment. I was one step away from wearing white gloves and turning the pages with tweezers.

The only other book I owned this thick and dense was the Church-issued Bible with my name embossed on the cover —and it just collected dust on my shelf. Not my Guinness Books. They grew tattered and dog-eared from overuse. I'd flip repeatedly to pictures of the World's Largest Pizza, the World's Smallest Horse, the World's Heaviest Twins, and a much younger Arnold Schwarzenegger in his beach-swinger Mr. Universe days. If they had made plastic action figures of the Guinness folks, I would have collected them and kept them lined up on a shelf in my bedroom.

I'd sometimes flex my own muscles in the bathroom mirror to imitate Arnold's Guinness pose. This was before his acting career took off, and in the photo he seems to be flexing on a sun-drenched beach, standing on a very small white towel in a tight bikini swimsuit. He's all shiny and lumpy, and with his fifty-eight-inch chest measurement, he's described by Guinness as "the most perfectly developed man in the history of the world."

More often than Arnold, I turned to Shridhar Chillal, the very serious man with the very serious fingernails curling up from his fingertips into long, bony loops. Though he may not have been the most perfectly developed man in the world, his fingernails were something to behold; and he was immortalized in the same pages as Arnold and poor Charles Osborne, the hiccup guy. He was right there next to the woman with the thirteen-inch waist, William Fuqua the Living Statue, and the man with the beard of bees cascading down his torso. He was famous.

God, I wanted to be like him.

I fixated on lots of records but especially loved the black-and-white photographs of record holders. The World's Heaviest (not Fattest) Twins, Benny and Billy McCrary, dressed the same and drove identical motorcycles—looking like two bearded June bugs riding a couple of fleas. Michael Barban posed on his pogo stick in a parking lot outside an apartment building. He bounced for a record eighteen hours on this pogo stick. *Eighteen hours!* The lists of names and accomplishments, the pictures of these people, filled my head until my skull was congested with Guinness.

• • •

I felt rather freakish as a child. Years of sickness as a toddler made me thin and weak, but when I began to recover, I grew at a rapid pace, until at age ten I inhabited a 5'7", 160-pound frame that just seemed too large for my personality. I felt awkward, clumsy, and totally misfit for childhood. In Guinness I found people who had become heroes and freaks by both accident and intention, and I could tell that nobody really knew what to make of them either. They didn't fit into easy categories of understanding. They couldn't be casually dismissed or embraced.

I was taller than most of my teachers and figured to be at least as smart as a couple of them. They never seemed to understand me and often ended up moving my desk into the hall. When I was out in public, adults regularly confused me for a teenager. I played Little League baseball and the coaches had to order special uniforms. When I played football the officials made me wear strips of white athletic tape on my shoulders to mark me as overweight. I was also required to produce identification to get the child's price at the movie theater. My dad had to bribe the amusement park employees so they'd let me play in the plastic ball pit with Matt. Though just eighteen months younger, he was always half my size, always handsome and charming and secure in his identity.

Not me. My body was an accident that set me apart from my friends, my brother, and myself. None of it was my fault really. I didn't intend to be an enormous child, didn't intend to be freakish and bookish. My rapid growth couldn't be predicted or avoided. It just happened. But people have told me, in confidence, after a few drinks, that I used to frighten them.

Lisping and swaying from alcohol, they will say (somewhat accusingly with a finger wagging at me) that I was big and scary, and that I bullied them or teased them unmercifully in elementary school. Most of these incidents are conveniently absent from my memory.

As much as I want to, I can't make excuses by telling them that I always felt somehow smaller than the other children, or at least different. This doesn't mean much. They probably felt the same way for different reasons. But in the pages of Guinness I found people famous for their big bodies, notorious for their scars and marks, forgiven for their excesses, men like Robert Earl Hughes, who weighed 378 pounds at the age of ten and was buried in a coffin the size of a piano case, hoisted by a steel crane into his grave. I was normal compared to him.

Each of them attained a heroic immortal status. Most of these Guinness folks weren't pop stars or beauty queens or anything like Arnold. They weren't wealthy or powerful. They might've even been good-hearted bullies in school like me. They too might have been misunderstood and scribbled portraits of possible selves in the margins of their schoolbooks, imagining their inevitable ascendance to the rank of World Record Holder, consistently ignoring the teacher's homework instructions and acting up, acting out, acting *bad*. To me they were flawed heroes and thus seemed more real, more believable, and more human.

• • •

Children often stare at me today, and I imagine that my son, Malcolm, will soon do the same—in much the way I stared in awe at *my* father. Dad seemed almost otherworldly—mainly because of his size. Part of the reason I get stares is my own fault—the buzz-cut hair, earrings, and jagged scar on my right cheek. But most of it is my present size—six feet, four inches, 260 pounds. Not huge any longer, not giant—probably a little overweight. Every now and then a kid at the grocery store will still look up at me and, right in front of his father, say, "He's bigger than you, isn't he, Dad?"

Malcolm likes to treat my body like a jungle gym or some other kind of climbing apparatus. He wants to hang from my arms, wants to be lifted up in my hands and tumbled around in the air. Sometimes he will pitch his body in ways that suggest he has either no regard for his own safety or complete trust in my ability to protect him. Sometimes I barely catch him before he hits the floor.

I know how he feels, though. There is something both monstrous and heroic, both freakish and fascinating, about a person so much bigger than you, five times your size sometimes. That's how my father always seemed to me. We'd go to the swimming pool in the summer, and Matt and I would take turns climbing on his back and riding him around like some kind of trained whale. His skin was cool and fish-slippery, and he would dive down beneath the noisy surface with one of us hanging from his neck and cruise the silent pool bottom for a few seconds before breaching again.

• • •

Matt would say that I make too much of my size. He'd tell me that I think too much, that I make myself crazy with it, and he'd be right. I make too much of everything. That's why I'm telling this story. Sometimes I feel like my memories are this rangy, wily herd of miniature horses, a roiling, knee-high sea of hides and rumps and tawny manes, and my job is to run around the edges, jabbing at the little beasts with an electrified steel prod, trying to keep them all moving in the same direction. Every now and then one of them gets loose, and I follow it for a while, crossing horizon lines, trying to bring it back into the fold. Sometimes I just watch it go.

Hiccoughing. **The longest recorded attack of hiccoughs is that afflicting Charles Osborne (b. 1894) of Anthon, Iowa, from 1922 to date. He contracted it when slaughtering a hog. His**

first wife left him and he is unable to keep in his false teeth. (1980, 43)

As a kid, on one level I liked to imagine myself pictured in the pages of Guinness. World's Largest Ten-Year-Old, Biggest Hands for a Child Under Twelve (I could already palm a basketball), World Record Holder for Consuming Breakfast Cereal, Most Injuries on One Side of a Body. Ben Douglas and I had candy-eating contests—my moment of glory coming when I crammed an entire box of Hot Tamales cinnamon chews into my mouth and nearly suffocated.

I too wanted to be the kind of hero-freak that would attract the attention of Norris McWhirter, editor and compiler of the Guinness Books.* As if they were aware of this, the doctors would pull out growth charts and show my parents how I was in something like the 125th percentile in both height and weight. I was *off* the charts while Matt was barely *on* them.

On another level I just wanted to be normal like my brother.

I could've handled being roughly the same size as he was, maybe just a little taller. I didn't want to linger in Matt's imagi-

---

☞ The *Guinness Book of World Records* was founded, with sponsorship from the Guinness Brewery, in 1955 and edited by the twin brothers Ross and Norris McWhirter. Both brothers were politically active and outspoken on social issues in Great Britain. Ross McWhirter was murdered in 1975 by an IRA assassin, and Norris McWhirter, who continued to edit the books until 1986, died while playing tennis at his home in April 2004. It is probably safe to assume that much of the quirky voice and wry sense of humor found in the Guinness Books can be attributed to one or both of the McWhirter brothers.

nation or the minds of fellow children as the embodiment of Bully or Freak. It was as if my body was overcompensating for the sickness of my early childhood, piling on pounds and inches, coursing with hormones until my feet ached constantly from growing pains and my skin broke out in a relief map of pimples. There was nothing I could do. My body seemed to develop a will of its own, and it was the Guinness Books that gave me an escape—a strange and seductive escape into the territory of the imagination.

Heaviest Twins.

The heaviest ever were the performers Billy Leon and Benny Loyd McCrary, alias Billy and Benny McGuire (born December 7, 1946) of Hendersonville, North Carolina. In November, 1978, they were weighed at 743 lbs. (Billy) and 723 lbs. (Benny) and had 84-inch waists. Billy died of heart failure on July 14, 1979. He was buried in a square coffin with a total weight of over 1,000 lbs. in Hendersonville. A hydraulic lift was needed to lower the coffin to its final resting place. (1980, 22)

Bond, Closest.

Matt was only a year behind me in school, and he seemed to be everywhere that I was. There was no separation between us. In the halls, on the playground, in the library, after school, on the bus, at home—Matt was right there. It often felt like I had a twin. We were supposed to be buddies, playmates, partners in crime. We were supposed to look out for each other. But whatever the connection twins have that allows them to share everything from clothes to careers, whatever the bond that spawns those stories of sympathetic pain and suffering— Matt and I just didn't have it.

There were problems from the beginning. His birth was positively *apocalyptic* for me, and I wanted my parents to put him back where they found him. When he was just a baby, Mom used to put Matt in a playpen in the kitchen while she worked. One day he was rolling around in there, just getting used to the feel of his legs, and he managed to pull himself up to a standing position by holding onto the sides of the playpen. Mom got all excited and cheered for him, clapping her hands and saying, "Oh, you're such a big boy, such a good baby-baby."

Matt was giggling and babbling, and Mom was going nuts over him, and I heard it all from the other room. I was playing quietly with my Legos like Mom had asked me to do, and I tried to ignore it, tried to be good. But it was too much. Something had to be done. I just couldn't let this pass. It was a matter of survival.

I thundered into the kitchen, a Lego piece clutched in one hand, and stopped in front of the playpen. I gazed up at Mom as if to remind her that this was all her fault—and then I punched baby Matt square in the nose.

This is *my* house.

That didn't last long. Mom spanked me with a wooden spoon because she couldn't bear to do it with her own hand, and that thing stung like nothing else. Eventually I learned that I wasn't in charge. Still, Mom had to quit taking us to the grocery store and letting us ride in the cart after I dropped a jar of applesauce on Matt's soft little head.

. . .

Somehow Matt and I managed to find common ground, ways to be friends *and* brothers. Typically this endeavor involved firing our Wrist-Rocket slingshots at the barn swallows Dad had authorized us to kill, hunting for crawdads in the creek behind the house, or basically anything that got us outside and kept us busy.

Most often we were together on our bikes or Big Wheels or this kick-ass chopper-tricycle Dad built for us. We were known throughout the neighborhood for roaming great distances on our bikes, and my parents often received calls from friends reporting sightings.

There are photographs—the big brother and the little brother—wearing khaki shorts, knee-high cowboy boots, and hats, riding our twin yellow Schwinn Scramblers with the banana seats, and each one of us beams a big, toothy grin. We look so happy together.

. . .

In the photo of the World's Heaviest Twins from my Giant 1980 Super-Edition, Benny and Billy McCrary sit atop their matching motorcycles. They wear matching black shirts and matching black-and-white checkered pants. They wear the same boots, same dark sunglasses, and same white cowboy hats. Each of them sports a thick neck, beard, and mustache, and Benny—the smaller brother—is smiling big for the camera. Billy doesn't really smile. His face looks more pained than anything.

Their checkered pants bulge out so much it looks as if they've each stuffed a couple of pillows down the front, and the motorcycles could be toy motorcycles they're so small by comparison. You can just barely make out the rear wheels. The twins seem to be posing on their bikes in the parking lot of a Holiday Inn.

I can't be sure about some things in the picture, but that doesn't stop me from speculating. I find myself imagining things about Benny and Billy—all in an effort to understand something more about *my* brother and our relationship. I know it sounds a bit strange, but this picture of the twins is a window into another world, and for a split second, it reminds me of some of those old photos with Matt and me on our bikes, but in a peripheral, out-of-body sort of way. That's the thing about the Guinness Books. They're full of these little passages into that wild, bushy territory of the mind. Once I step through, strangely enough the path always seems to lead me back home—back to my father, my brother, and me.

• • •

Matt and I were brothers on bikes, but we didn't have the same sort of bond that the McCrary twins seem to have had. I don't think we've ever been as close as each of us hoped we would be. We could never set a World Record together. There's just too much other shit that would get in the way. But sometimes I think if we could rise above all that, we might be able to accomplish something beautiful, or spectacular, or unbelievable.

Benny and Billy seem like two fun-loving brothers who enjoyed spending time together, the very picture of brotherhood. But I can't help but wonder about some of the gaps in the Guinness entry. It's always about the gaps for me. That's where the stories sprout. What sorts of performers were the twins? What kind of professional relationship did they have? Did they simply show up for events and ride around on their motorcycles?

I like to imagine them performing spectacular stunts, maybe some impressive figure eights or, better yet, suspended in one of those twirling metal cages where they ride furiously in tight loops like giant hamsters, or maybe riding on the Wall of Death with Speedy Babbs. Afterward they jump their bikes over a row of junked cars, showgirls, or Holstein cows. They wear capes and shiny helmets.

I can just imagine the scene. It comes to me like a vision. We have gathered here today . . . at this county airstrip . . . under a blazing yellow sun . . . to bear witness to the Fabulous

McCrary Brothers. The PA system thunders with "Free Bird" by Lynyrd Skynyrd as the brothers take a couple of warm-up laps. The first few chords of "Smoke on the Water" rise like a tide, and the brothers come racing past the grandstand where I'm seated. They perform intricate, high-speed weave maneuvers, and the capacity crowd whips into a frenzy of anticipation. Men, women, and children scream at the top of their lungs.

Benny McCrary—the fearless one—circles back around and moves full speed down the airport runway. He climbs carefully up onto the seat of his bike until he's standing with one foot on the gas tank and one on the seat, his hands still on the bars. This was a trick Matt and I used to do for fun on our own motorcycles, but Benny takes it to another level.

Slowly and carefully, Benny lifts himself to a standing position, hands raised in a Jesus pose, zooming past us, balanced on the bike like some sort of Mongolian horse warrior riding into battle.

Billy—the bigger brother—moves in behind on his bike and lays back on his seat, hooking his toes around the motorcycle's handlebars and dangling his hands dangerously close to the pavement. The wind riffles his trademark checkered pants and tugs his shirt loose, exposing his white belly.

The crowd erupts into thunderous applause.

The brothers do victory laps on their bikes and sign autographs for children.

I want to believe all of this. But something tells me this isn't how it went. I suspect their performances were more *spectacle* than *spectacular*—the kinds of things that can be called "stunts" only because they are being performed by seven-hundred-pound twins. I mean how fast could those bikes really go with that much weight? Their shows must have been more like slow-motion dances of fat and cowboy hats.

I don't know the truth, and I'm not sure I want to know.

There's something about these guys, something I both envy and pity. I want to see them at the height of their performing careers, learn more about their relationship, before the whole wrestling thing. What happened there? Maybe something came between them. Maybe a Guinness Record wasn't enough. How do two brothers so close, so similar, carve out separate identities? What divides the two besides a few pounds and some time between their births?

These are the questions I keep asking myself.

Matt and I seemed to develop our personalities in opposition to each other, almost like defense mechanisms, and I've always been both jealous of and mystified by men who maintain strong and healthy relationships with their brothers. I find myself trying to puzzle things out. I want to compare notes and observations. I want to know how they do it. It seems like something I should be able to teach my son.

Suppose Benny—the smaller brother—just didn't care about the same things that Billy did, just didn't have the same goals. Suppose he had no interest in wearing checkered pants and riding a motorcycle. He didn't want to be a performer and just wanted to stay home in Hendersonville and open an auto parts store. There may have been all sorts of rifts between them, small disagreements and petty differences we don't know about, but somehow, through it all, they stayed together. Perhaps it's easy to explain their bond as a natural outcome of being raised with a twin your entire life. But I want to believe it's more than genetics or biology. I want to believe that Matt and I could've been a world-famous motorcycle stunt team. We'd have been the Flying Church Brothers, and we'd have worn red capes and blue helmets and performed at county fairs and carnivals too.

• • •

In addition to their careers as a motorcycle stunt team, Benny and Billy tried their hands at professional wrestling. If I had a time machine, I'd go back for one of their matches. That would be something to see, something I'm sure I could learn a lot from. I can understand the allure of the professional wrestling world—the money, the lights, the fame, the chance to tangle with the likes of "King" Harley Race, "The Natural" Butch Reed, Ric Flair, Dusty Rhodes, Kamala the Ugandan Giant, or some other icon of that world. What context besides Guinness rewards you so handsomely for such freakish behavior? But I bet I could also learn something about teamwork and brother-hood.

I imagine the twins, decked out in supersize denim overalls, lumbering around the ring, bouncing off the turnbuckles and slamming into other wrestlers, smothering them with their great masses of flesh and denim. A woman in the front row yells, "Kill him, Billy. Kill him!" as the twins hook elbows in a slow-motion twirl that whips Benny across the ring into the torso of an unsuspecting Chief Wahoo McDaniel. The Chief sprawls out on the mat in an exaggerated spill of flesh. Billy runs full speed and flops on top of him. The referee slides in and pounds out a three-count on the mat as Benny cheers Billy on from the corner. When it's over the brothers stand victorious in the ring, hands clasped over their heads, as the crowd roars approval.

As much as it pains me to admit it, Matt and I would never have made a good wrestling tag team. We're too mismatched, too dissimilar, too competitive for this kind of teamwork. We didn't have a close enough bond. The only way we would've ever been in the wrestling ring together is if we were battling each other in some kind of David versus Goliath gimmick match. Of course I would've been the heavily favored and much-hated Goliath, and Matt would've been a David-like Jimmy "Superfly" Snuka, delighting the crowd by leaping gracefully from the turnbuckles and flying around the ring.

• • •

It's clear that Billy—the older, bigger brother—died in 1979 and Benny erected an enormous monument in his honor, but it's not clear exactly how Billy died. Several sources I found (most of them online wrestling fan magazines) mention complications or injuries resulting from a motorcycle stunt gone awry, but they don't say specifically what happened.

The Giant 1980 Super-Edition of the Guinness Book, printed one year after his death, says he died of "heart failure" —and it's just my romantic and jealous mind that wants to interpret this as saying he died of a "broken heart" because he and his brother were never as close as they should have been, never as connected as everyone expected. Perhaps the brothers never liked each other at all, and were more like Matt and me than I think. Maybe Benny just broke down under the pressure of keeping up appearances.

I like the mystery, even if it is at least partly manufactured by my own ignorance. I don't want to know exactly how Billy died because, in the gaps, I can already imagine the wounded brother staggering away from the wreckage. This is the way it goes.

The back wheel of his fallen bike spins furiously in the air. The crowd pitches forward on their seats. Steppenwolf's "Magic Carpet Ride" blares from the PA. Benny drops his own bike on the pavement and runs to his brother. He's just a few steps away as Billy stumbles, reaches one hand out, clutching at his chest with the other, and falls into Benny's arms. Both men go down in a heap, their shiny helmets rolling across the pavement. Benny sits up and lifts Billy's head onto his lap, stroking his brother's hair and humming old country songs their grammy used to sing. He holds him like that until the sirens come and his twin heart stops pumping.

Piano Smashing.

The record time for demolishing an upright piano and passing the entire wreckage through a circle 9 inches in diameter is 1 minute 37 seconds by six members of the Tinwald Rugby Football Club, Ashburton, New Zealand, led by David Young on November 6, 1977.

Anthony Fukes, Mike Newman, Terry Cullington and Malcolm Large smashed a piano *with bare hands*, passing all wreckage through a 9-inch circle, in 7 minutes in Nottingham, England, on June 6, 1977, a record equaled by the foursome of C. Crain, R. Crain, O. Richards and M. Cording on December 16, 1978, also in Nottingham. (1980, 476)

Smashing, Bare Hand.

I imagine that this piano-smashing business is some kind of ceremonial act, a ritualistic and symbolic smashing of music or the arts or namby-pamby intellectuals. Perhaps it's a male-bonding experience shared by all rugby clubs, passed down for generations, a way to unite the team against a common (and easily defeated) foe—the goddamn smarmy piano.

Arggh, bloody cursed piano! I hate your flat C and your pathetic little hammers!

I see a drunken scrum of rugby lads in kilts mowing like a wood chipper through an upright Steinway, and for some reason they all talk in an exaggerated Scottish accent and smack mugs of bitter beer together in celebration.

I played the piano. Not well. But that was mainly because I never practiced and my hands wouldn't cooperate with my brain. I didn't enjoy the piano, but I don't remember ever having the urge to smash it into little bits with my bare hands and pass it through a hoop. Furthermore, who established the nine-inch circle as the standard piano-smashing and passing circumference? Did they try an eight-inch circle or maybe a ten-inch? Is there a piano-smashing hoop that bartenders keep on hand for spontaneous smashing events?

This whole thing is so typically male, isn't it? Women knit. They make babies and throw pots and plant gardens. Men smash stuff.

Sure it's an oversimplification, but the truth is, from the time I was a little boy, I've loved smashing things—taking something whole or complete and rendering it into shards, chunks, or fragments. Lightbulbs. Plates. The amputated screen from an old television. Matt's toys. Mom's flowerpots. Memories. Records. The walls in the garage. My cousin Cindy's snail collection.

I took a natural history museum class one summer that had something to do with astronomy. We learned some stuff about the solar system and the big bang theory, but the highlight for me was when the teacher brought in a vat of liquid nitrogen.

I'd brought a blue rubber racquetball Dad gave me and watched with awe as the teacher plucked the ball off the table with a pair of tongs, and dipped it in the vat for a few seconds. He pulled the ball out, cupped it in his gloved hand, and whipped it at the floor, reducing it to a crushed scatter of frozen blue chips.

As the teacher took a long-stemmed rose from one of the girls and dipped it into the liquid nitrogen, I couldn't help but imagine plunging my hand into the vat, holding it for a few seconds, brandishing it with dramatic flair, and then smashing it on the table. I saw little chunks of finger and bone splintering off and skittering across the table like ice chips. I figured it wouldn't really hurt until the hand started to thaw.

While I was lost in my own head, the teacher pulled the rose from the vat, and the little girls squealed as he tapped it on the table. The red petals shattered into a thousand pieces, spraying our lab table with perfumed confetti, but I couldn't stop thinking about my shattered frozen hand. They'd probably have to send me home with my fingers in a plastic cup, and I'd rattle them around in the cup until they started to thaw and quit making noise.

Once when I was in college my computer crashed and gobbled up a paper I had just finished writing. In a spontaneous fit of rage I brought my size thirteen boot down hard on my wooden desk chair, reducing it to a pile of scrap wood. I instantly felt better. So good in fact that I considered purchasing a few old chairs and keeping them around for just such cathartic occasions.

Is the urge to smash more nature or nurture? Hard to say, but it was certainly part of my childhood. I see it in my own son too. Sometimes Malcolm just can't resist the urge to destroy his carefully constructed Lego towers or wood-block castles. The first time we gave him an Easter egg, he couldn't stop himself from crushing it to a pulp, pressing his thumbs through the shell, and sinking them into the white and yolk. I haven't taught him these things. He just does them.

Of course Dad gave me my share of lessons in smashing stuff. After our family moved into a house near the University of Kansas campus, we decided to do some kitchen remodeling that involved removing an entire wall. This was something I imagined would require precise and detailed measuring and cutting, perhaps a team of carpenters with tools in large plastic boxes. I thought we'd have to dismantle the wall one piece at a time, being careful not to disturb important structural elements. But when Matt and I came upstairs one morning to help Dad, he just handed each of us a hammer.

"What's this for?" I asked.

"For taking out that wall," he said, as if it was a stupid question. "Like this." He took the hammer from me, swung his arm back, and embedded the claw in the wall. "See?" he said as he wedged the hammer in and popped out a chunk of drywall. White dust floated through the air and settled on the floor.

"Go nuts," he said.

Matt grinned and sunk his hammer into the wall. It made a dull *thwump* sound, and he had to twist the claw to pull it out. He giggled, and it was an involuntary sort of noise—a little burp of satisfaction.

I raised my hammer in the air and slammed it into the wall over and over and over again. We pounded into the soft drywall and popped out chunks until there was nothing left but the battered two-by-four studs, and then we ripped those out too, knocking them loose with a sledgehammer and piling the pine bones up in the driveway. I'd never realized that remodeling could be so much fun.

• • •

So perhaps those piano-hating rugby boys, all hopped up on testosterone and adrenaline, were simply indulging in the time-honored male tradition of smashing stuff. Perhaps it was a cathartic sort of thing they did after a particularly frustrating match. I imagine it gave them the kind of emotional release that sends a man home unburdened, unfettered, and allows him the patience to towel-dry the head of a small child, cook a meal for ungrateful teenagers, repair a leaky faucet, maybe even stitch a Halloween costume or two.

• • •

My father had talented hands. He played the piano and trombone as a boy, and every now and then, he'd sit down at the piano in our living room and tap out a few notes. He had long fingers that moved with spider-like agility over the keys.

Dad's hands looked as big as the sea monsters in my *How to Draw Sea Monsters* tracing book. They were five-fingered giant squid that could swallow you whole. Matt and I didn't get spanked a lot. We found ways not to get caught, especially when getting caught meant dealing with one of Dad's hands. It wasn't that he hit us so hard. It was just that one of his hands seemed to cover my entire rear end. It was like he was spanking not just your bottom but your whole *body.*

When Dad woke me up in the morning for school, sitting down on the edge of my bed and resting his hand on my back, it felt like a warm, fleshy mammal grabbing my shoulders, squeezing my neck, pulling me out of the watery haze of sleep. It may sound strange, but sometimes I wondered what it's like for a big boy with small parents, a father with tiny hands. Would this boy have a different understanding of parental authority?

• • •

My father has hypnotic powers. At least that's what's been said . . . well, really not so much *said* as implied. A few words leaked out here and there, released like air from a balloon. I think it was my uncle Rick who first let it slip in front of me. I'm not really sure, but I latched onto the idea and wouldn't let it go.

Dad can hypnotize people.

I believed this. It seemed right.

There was more to the story, though. Something unspoken involving my mother, and it wasn't good. Though I'd never been told this directly, I had the feeling that my father had hypnotized, or tried to hypnotize, my mother. I'd occasionally ask Dad about it until he'd talk in the abstract about how you can induce a trancelike state by swinging something like a pocket watch and speaking in slow, deliberate tones. I asked him to show me, but he never did. He'd say it was something I didn't need to know, and then he'd change the subject.

That's the way it always worked in our family. Nothing specific ever said, nothing really revealed. Just vaguely intriguing hints, the kind of thing that stirs the imagination of a young boy. Living in my family is often like living in an Ernest Hemingway story without the booze. Everyone is extremely sober and austere on the surface and hiding painful secrets and stories underneath. There's lots of talk about fishing and guns.

I often thought that if I just read between the lines more, I might get the real story. But I still don't know quite what to make of this whole hypnotism thing. My dad does have a certain sway over people, an undeniable charm, and even sophistication. But he also tells dirty jokes and drinks shitty beer. Hypnotism? It seems too subtle for Dad. In Boy Scouts, during a highly appropriated and simplified version of an Indian naming ceremony, Dad was dubbed "Bull of the Bittersweet" by his peers. Once when he was being recruited for a business venture, one of the principal partners said he needed a "five-hundred-pound gorilla to go in there and throw some people around." That was Dad.

• • •

I remember once being racked with a wicked case of hiccups. It was nothing like what Charles Osborne suffered for at least fifty-seven years, but they were the kind that don't go away and seem to suck all the air out of your body, the kind of hiccups that make you want to cry they hurt so bad.

Dad sits down on my bed and, with a sympathetic voice, says that if I hold my breath for an hour the hiccups will go away. I squeeze my mouth shut and count to ten in my head before I realize he is playing a joke on me, before I understand that to hold my breath for an hour is to kill myself. Dad laughs and points at me as I puff my breath out.

You might think this is one of those things only a small child would do. But later in life, when I am thirteen or fourteen, I burn my leg on the tailpipe of my motorcycle. The flesh peels off in brown flakes. Little bits of skin stick to the metal. Dad calls the burn unit at the hospital. When he gets off the phone, he says to keep an eye out for red streaks and swelling.

"If you see that," he says, "they'll have to *amputate.*"

AMPUTATE! The word rattles around inside my skull. Dad leaves me alone for a couple of hours while he runs some errands—only that word to keep me company. When he returns I am in near hysterics, pointing at the obvious red streaks in my leg and crying for the limb I think I have already lost. Never, never again will I wear shorts on a motorcycle. Dad laughs at me nervously and says that he was only kidding, the nurse on the phone didn't mention a word about amputation.

"It was just a joke," he says. "I thought you knew. A joke."

• • •

Even though Dad had those enormous, authoritative hands, they were always soft and warm. When I was a boy I liked to hold his paw in my lap and play with his wedding ring, twisting it around his thick finger and wedging my own fingers in between his. Sometimes he'd squeeze his fingers together, trapping mine.

Dad did tricks with his hands too. He'd make alligator and turtle shapes and funny little mouths or flying fish. He'd hide coins in his hands and make it seem as if they'd fallen from your ear. Not only did he have long fingers but his palms were also wide and deeply creased. Just one of his hands could wrap from one side of your rib cage to the other and unleash merciless tickle attacks.

After our baths at night, Mom would often plunk us down in Dad's lap with a towel, and he'd slowly massage our heads until our hair was dry or we had fallen asleep in his arms. I loved the feel of his hands working over my skull.

Now I have my father's hands, and I've passed them on to my son. They're the hands that allowed me to palm a basketball at age eleven and dunk a basketball when I was still under six feet tall. I could just jump up and push the ball over the rim with one hand. They're the same hands I nervously twisted as a fifth-grader, bending my fingers into pretzels and showing off my double-jointed abilities by flexing the tips, the same ones I use now to punctuate my sentences with authority when I talk.

They're the same hands that cupped my newborn son's body and carried him to his mother while the doctors stitched up her womb and belly, the same hands that gave him his first sponge bath and cradled his soft, misshapen head while Rachel shook uncontrollably from the anesthesia and her teeth chattered like castanets.

Longest Finger Nails.

The longest finger nail ever grown is one of 25 1/2 inches, grown in 13 years by Romesh Sharma of Delhi, India, measured on February 15, 1979.

The longest known set of nails now belong to the left hand of Shridhar Chillal, 41, of Poona, India. The 5 nails have been uncut since 1952, and by February 23, 1979, they had reached a total measured length of 92 1/2 inches, including a thumbnail 23.2 inches long. Human nails normally grow from cuticle to cutting length in from 117 to 138 days. (1980, 38)

Commitment, Longest.

In the photograph of Shridhar in my 1980 Super-Edition of the Guinness Book, he does not look directly at the camera. He clearly doesn't see himself as a freak. His thick black hair is combed up and back. No sideburns to speak of. His lips are full, but he does not smile. He's a young man, but you can see that he takes himself very seriously. He has the dark, piercing eyes and swarthy good looks of a silent film star.

His right arm is crossed beneath his left, which he holds up for the camera. He wears a square watch and a wristband of some kind. His fingers are spread wide, and long, bony serpents curl out from the tips. The thumbnail is the thickest of them all, and it loops up and back down to the soft pad, 23.2 inches of bony growth.

When I was in fifth grade, I kept a corner of my own thumbnail long and sharp—because there was this spot in my gums, just behind my upper right bicuspid, where the nerves ran close to the surface. During class sometimes, bored to death, I'd press my thumbnail hard into those nerves just to feel the hot, sharp pain that surged through my whole body like an electrical current.

It's hard to say why I liked it—maybe because it was so precise, so focused, and I needed this certainty to cope with the creeping awareness of the self I'd seen reflected in the eyes of others. Perhaps I was so used to living with objectless anxiety that I needed some pain that was concentrated, identifiable, and finite. It was a pain I could turn on and off with just the touch of a fingernail—unlike the emotions I felt surrounding my own adolescence.

• • •

Commitment seems of utmost importance if you want to make the Guinness Books, and I admire Shridhar Chillal's commitment to growing his fingernails. Think what it must have taken to do this.*

By 1980 Shridhar had already spent twenty-seven years developing a single overarching identity, one dominant self-image. He chose to be that way, to allow himself to be considered freakish by some standards. He used his body as a vehicle for self-expression, and set himself apart from the normal

☞ As of 1998, Shridhar Chillal was still the record holder for longest fingernails, having been so for the last eighteen years. I found a recent picture of him on the Internet, and the difference in photographs is striking. In the most recent one, he stands sort of slumped to the side, with his left hand raised in the air. He wears a white shirt, but the tails have come untucked. His hair is flecked with gray, and he just looks tired—nothing like the proud Shridhar in my 1980 book. His nails hang down past his knees, and the thumbnail is curled into a tight spiral the size of a dinner plate. According to Guinness, he has suffered permanent disfigurement to his hand and nerve damage to his ear. He hasn't had a full night's sleep in decades. The website with his picture advertises a unique opportunity. Shridhar has decided to sell his record-setting fingernails, and whoever put up the site has suggested that the best way to display them would be with a life-size statue of Shridhar carved out of granite, or possibly wax, with the fingernails attached. I tried to contact the individual listed on the website but have yet to receive a response.

people. Was it because he hoped that someone might one day consider him heroic, some kid from Kansas with an unnatural attraction to his photograph? I doubt it, but there has to be some reward, doesn't there?

He'd have to tend to those nails, keep them moist and soft somehow. He'd have to baby them. You can't just ignore fingernails like these. He'd have to sand them with a fine-grain paper—nothing too coarse—and maybe paint them with a couple of coats of clear polish. He'd have to commit himself to them completely. Maybe his wife sewed a protective silk bag for nights out on the town and a cotton bag for quiet evenings at home. She might have quilted the inside and stuffed it with

goose feathers. Maybe she worked two jobs so they could survive, and Shridhar cobbled together a meager salary from freak shows, mall appearances, and the occasional Guinness TV special. I don't know anything for sure. What mattered, though, was the commitment to this image. I can't help but wonder what sources of validation and affirmation he finds for his fingernails. What does his family think? How does he eat or use the bathroom? Can he drive? I still have questions. I will always have questions.

Lightest Humans. **Edward C. Hagner (1892–1962), alias Eddie Masher, is alleged to have weighed only 48 lbs. at a height of 5 feet 7 inches. He was also known as "the Skeleton Dude." (1980, 20)**

There are so many things we don't know about the Guinness characters—the minutiae of daily life with a twenty-three-inch thumbnail, eight feet of hair, or the compulsion to eat a bicycle.* Maybe they have children too and define themselves as parents and spouses, teachers and plumbers, fishermen and housewives.

They could have extremely pedestrian and domestic squabbles. Maybe Benny McCrary got a rash from his checkered pants and blamed it on Billy's eco-friendly soap. Maybe the two of them weren't talking like they used to right before Billy died. We'd never know from the books we read, the shows we watch, or the stories we tell. We'd never know from the scattered and fragmented images we see.

Robert Earl Hughes might have a thing about his sock stripe matching his T-shirt. He may never have imagined himself a World Record Holder. Perhaps he was a disappointment to his parents. He could have places on his body he hasn't seen for years. This isn't so glamorous. Maybe the eight-foot giant spends all of his money on music lessons and soccer leagues for the little ones. His wife has probably grown tired of altering his pants and resents the cobwebs in the vaulted ceilings of their home.

They could all be more human than we'd like to admit. They could have oversize children who frighten the neighbors. Maybe Eddie Masher, the Skeleton Dude, has a sickly child who seems to be wasting away and medical bills through the

---

Bicycle. 15 days by Monsieur "Mangetout" (M. Lotito), in the form of tires and metal filings, at Evry, France, March 17–April 2, 1977. No further entries in this category will be accepted (1980, 489).

roof. Maybe his wife left him for a male gymnast who lives in a duplex and has a pommel horse in his yard. Maybe Eddie drove by there the other day and stopped to watch his wife's new boyfriend executing perfect scissor kicks on the pommel horse, his arms rippling with muscle and his legs just a blur of movement, almost like the wings of a hummingbird.

Rarest Disease.

Kuru, or laughing sickness, afflicts only the Fore Tribe of eastern New Guinea and is 100% fatal. This was formally attributed to the cannibalistic practice of eating human brains. (1982, 42)

Commonest Diseases.

The commonest contagious illness in the world is coryza (acute nasopharyngitis) or the common cold. The case of the person most resistant to being affected by a cold was reported by the Medical Research Council Common Cold Unit, Salisbury, England, to be J. Brophy, who had only one mild reaction after being exposed 24 times. (1982, 42–43)

Boy, Bionic.

As a boy I was obsessed with the television series *The Six Million Dollar Man,* starring Lee Majors, in which they rebuild an injured astronaut named Steve with *bionic parts* and grant him all sorts of impressive new talents. Sure, part of it was that name, Steve Austin—so regal and heroic. I loved that we shared a first name. But it was more than that. I didn't want to be a sickly child; I wanted to be an astronaut too. I wanted to believe in bionics. I wanted to crush a baseball in my fist and leap over twelve-foot fences with ease.

The truth is I latched onto any cool TV hero named Steve. Dad would let me stay up late with him sometimes to watch *Hawaii Five-O,* with its dapper, anvil-haired protagonist, Steve McGarrett. He was so cool, so sharp, so well dressed. In the late seventies, early eighties, TV was populated with cool, mysterious, crime-fighting Steves.* But the Six Million Dollar Man was always special—even though I couldn't help but worry at times about less successful Four and Five Million Dollar Man prototype versions. What happened to those guys? Are they hidden away in some government hospital now, barely human at all, just some brains in vats hooked up to electrodes?

☞ Of course this has all changed, and now the name Steve is typically associated with sniveling weasel types in yellow sweaters and penny loafers, superficial sports jerks, or complete dorks. See *Beverly Hills 90210,* for example.

In the opening sequence of the TV show, we see Steve Austin's moon landing craft crash on a runway, rolling into a ball of flame and smoke and twisted metal. A panicked voice comes on: "He's breaking up. He's breaking up. He's breaking up." The camera jumps to Steve in the hospital. "We can rebuild him, we have the technology." And they do rebuild him —with a robotic arm, legs, and eyeball. They make him *bigger, stronger, faster.* He wears that stylish red jumpsuit and runs to the pulsing, beeping sound of bionic parts in action. Steve is just so damn cool. How can you not love him?

Part of the attraction was his name, part of it his looks and his dry wit. But the deeper reason I liked him was his tortured soul. This half man–half machine had been through the fire. His body had been broken—and then rebuilt by doctors, government doctors—and he seemed to spend his entire life battling evil Bigfoot robots built by the same government doctors. He was, in many ways, in a love-hate relationship with his rebuilt body, and I was a sickly child who needed to identify with angst-ridden bionic heroes named Steve. It was that simple.

• • •

Mom got used to my sickness and learned to see my fever convulsions coming. The doctors called them "febrile seizures." They started when I was nineteen months old, just after Matt was born, and lasted for a few years. The typical attack began with a nervous restlessness and glassy eyes. Suddenly my body would go rigid and I'd be catatonic on the carpet, my temperature spiking up to well over a hundred degrees. Mom would hold me tight in her arms and try to squeeze the fevers out of me. Sometimes she could stave them off or control them with aspirin and cold showers. Other times there was nothing she could do but watch me suffer.

The last and worst one happened when I was four and we were driving home from my grandparents' home in Western Kansas. Mom saw it coming just outside of Topeka—saw it in my eyes like she always did. Dad drove fast, but as soon as we got to the house I blacked out, convulsed, and didn't come out of it. That night they took me to the hospital, where doctors treated me with antibiotics and tested for brain damage. They sent me home and told my parents to watch out for epilepsy later in life. They said there was a good chance I had cooked something up there in my skull.

After that I never had another full-blown seizure, but I still ran fevers and hallucinated. My sinuses were regularly ravaged by infections. My body was rail thin. Dad says my knees looked like baseballs bulging out of the skin. An infection in my head caused blisters to break out on my face. A virus settled into my legs and I collapsed at school in front of the classroom sink.

• • •

It seems like I spent a lot of time in the doctor's office. Dr. Pete had white rubber-gloved fingers he crammed down my throat on a regular basis. The pills he gave me didn't seem to work. I was always sick, and the medicine worried me as much as my fevers. I took my pills regularly as prescribed. I did what the doctors and my parents said. I finished all the doses, even though I was convinced that I was ingesting not antibiotics but *antibionics.*

I worried that the pills kept me sick, somehow ruining any chance to run fast, crush things with my fist, or see extremely well out of one eye. By the time I turned six, I'd been on various *antibionics* off and on for almost a year and I just seemed to get sicker and sicker—confirming my worst suspicions about the medical profession.

Dr. Pete decided that they needed to remove my tonsils. *We can remove them,* a voice whispered. There was some stubborn infection in my head they couldn't get rid of. My parents simply wanted the sickness to stop. After the operation, I still ran fevers, but no blackouts, no visions. Every now and then I felt the pulsing light, the speeding of time. I felt just on the verge of seeing again—but the hallucinations never came.

• • •

Even though they occurred at such a young age, I do have spotty memories of my seizures. Some of them are more like impressions or sensations, the vague outlines of a memory. Others are frighteningly clear. I've read accounts from those who suffer from grand mal epileptic seizures. They experience something like what I felt in my fevered state—a strange sort of euphoria both exhilarating and terrifying, an elevation of the spirit to feelings of omniscience and pulsing, vibrating light effects, as if plugged into some eternal circuit.

In my febrile seizures I heard the electrochemical buzz of lightbulbs, saw them surge with energy. Red digital clock numbers spun like they were written on rolling wheels. Flash, flash, flash. Time beat faster. My eyes opened wide. I'd be awake—sort of. Not asleep. I'd rub my eyes, pressing my palms into the sockets—trying to squeeze the fever out. But there, above my bed, floated giant turds skewered with wooden toothpicks. They drifted over me, bouncing off the walls of my room, swelling from the heat in my brain, colliding with one another and spinning around, the sharp points of the toothpicks just barely missing my head. They were so real, I was surprised when they didn't leave shit stains on the walls.

Some fever dreams made more sense, but they were always still tinged with a terrifying euphoria. Elevated in my vision—almost godlike—I floated over our house, our neighborhood, and our town. I saw everything.

My father riding his motorcycle to work. Children smacking a tetherball round and round a pole at Hillcrest School. Julie Johnson walking her dalmatian dog. Doug Platz shooting baskets in his driveway. My mother driving meals-on-wheels to senior citizens in our station wagon. My brother pedaling furiously around the block in cowboy boots and shorts. My family seated at the dining room table.

I saw them all. And I watched the river swell slowly, creeping up its banks. I saw the loose stones gather on the mountains, building up to burst. I heard the grumbling of earthquakes beneath the surface. I knew the end was coming, the apocalypse was inevitable, but nobody heard me when I tried to warn them, and when the devastation hit—houses splintered like toothpick castles, churches pushed off their foundations, people sucked under a tide of mud and water and rocks—I could only watch from my fevered perch.

In the midst of my childhood hallucinations, I sometimes picked up a spoon from my nightstand and rang the juice glass Mom set out for me. She always came running to help. Dad stood in a cold shower, clutching my limp body to his chest. Mom checked the thermometer: *105 degrees*. Dad shivered from the cold, watched the water pour over his firstborn son.

He shielded my eyes and wiped his thumb over my face. This repeated baptism I received—fire from the fevers, cold from the water—seemed to initiate me into a darker, stranger world, where I would live for the rest of my life. My father's skin pimpled with goose bumps. His teeth chattered. This wasn't the only time. My mother bathed my head with a washcloth. And then my eyes opened finally, the tears came, and I was a normal boy again, still boiling with fever dreams but awake and alive—clutched tight in my father's hands.

Before I reached the age of four, I'd imagined the end of the world. I'd seen the apocalypse. And for the rest of my life, I'd wonder if it would come back again. Now I find myself worrying every time my son runs a fever that he will slip into a seizure and I will end up in the shower with him clutched in my arms. I worry that he will see the apocalypse too.

• • •

Maybe it was the hallucinations, but my childhood sickness nearly led me down a different spiritual path altogether. During a Christmas celebration at my grandparents' house, I was lying on the double-padded red carpet in the living room when a seizure hit. I could feel my head boiling, and soon I was nearly catatonic with the fever. Mom and Dad dragged me into bed in the pink guest room, dosed me up with Tylenol, and covered me with blankets.

I faded in and out of fever states and was drifting around the edges of full consciousness when my aunt came in to check on me. She sat down on the edge of the bed and began to pray over me, asking the Lord for his help in healing my sickness, begging his intervention; and for a few minutes I did actually

45

begin to feel better. She was so somber, so serious, I felt the Lord come into that room. I believed it could happen.

I even got up out of bed and returned to the living room, trying to participate in the festivities, trying to pretend that everything was okay and that God had stopped my fever. But this lasted only a few minutes before my temperature spiked again and I was reduced to a gibbering, shivering mess on the floor. Sometimes I wonder how my life might have changed had God actually healed me that night. Would I have believed more seriously? Would I have accepted his existence without question? It's doubtful, but still I wonder how close I came that night to a life of faith.

• • •

When I got better my parents took Matt and me to Southern California. We visited Disneyland, SeaWorld, the San Diego Zoo, but the highlight for me was a pilgrimage to Universal Studios. Of course I was happy with the *Jaws* simulation, the earthquake bridge and rockslide, but nothing confirmed my faith in the creative power of humanity like the bionics demonstration.

We packed into a theater and sat as close to the front as we could. The curtains opened, and this troop of bionic interns came out onstage wearing red jogging suits. They were young and peppy and reminded me of cheerleaders. They lifted cars and large appliances. They leaped over furniture with ease.

It was all rather impressive. But things didn't really start getting exciting until they asked for volunteers for a special part of the show. My hand shot into the air. Dad grabbed me in the armpits and hoisted me up above everyone around us. I waved my arms frantically, trying to get their attention. They held their hands to their brows, making exaggerated gestures in scanning the audience. It seemed to take forever for them to see me, but finally one of the bionic interns pointed at me and I scampered up on the stage.

They set me up on a motorcycle with a white screen behind it and told me the Bionic Man would be chasing me and I should act as if I was trying to escape. Then they pointed to a camera mounted in front of the bike and told me to watch for the red light. I gripped the handlebars and squeezed the gas tank with my thighs. The red light came on, and I leaned forward slightly.

The bike tilted left and right. The camera rolled, and another projector beamed an image on the screen behind me. I turned to see Steve Austin, the Bionic Man, running behind me in his red jogging suit. The music kicked in and the bionic beeping echoed through the theater. They let it all roll for a while, and I raced my bike, leaning into the turns, mugging for the camera.

When they were finished, they rewound the videotape and played it back on the big screen. There I was, a young, virile criminal on the lam from justice, and the Bionic Man was chasing me down, hunting me with his superpowers. I had gone from voyeur to star in seconds. The crowd cheered. Mom and Dad were so proud. Matt was so jealous, and I was just stupid with happiness—feeling something like religious ecstasy in the simulated presence of my hero, Steve Austin.

· · ·

That year I got out of the house more. I stretched my limbs, trying to gain back some of the childhood I'd lost. One day I was riding my bike—a chunky red bike with solid rubber tires, something Dad put together on Christmas Eve—down the neighbors' sloped oval driveway.

The garage door gaped open. My friend Ronnie Olson flew ahead of me. I followed, but something went wrong.

Fear washed over me like a sneeze, and my muscles went rigid. In a full-on flinch, I jammed on the coaster brakes and nothing happened. I was going too fast. At the last moment I jerked the handlebars slightly, trying to avoid the car, and slammed full speed into the galvanized steel guide track for the garage door.

The track peeled my cheek open and sliced into my brow just above my right eye. Ronnie said later that he could see my cheekbone through the mess. I didn't notice pain so much— just a lot of wetness and fear. Mrs. Olson pressed towels to my face. I didn't worry about the ragged flap of skin hanging loose. I worried about soaking the Olsons' washcloths—the nice yellow ones from the hall bathroom that nobody used— with blood.

Mom showed up, loaded me into the station wagon, and drove me to the emergency room yet again. From the hospital, the only image that stayed with me was a blue paper bib covering my eyes. My vision filtered through a hole in the bib, I saw the needle moving up and down through my cheek flesh. I felt nothing from the anesthetic, remember nothing of the doctor lecturing my parents. While she sutured my face, she scolded Mom and Dad for letting a four-year-old loose on a bike, scolded them for being bad parents. "It's too dangerous for him to be riding a bike at this age," she said, and when it was over my wound bloomed with stiff black stitches.

It's still hard for my parents to talk about this, difficult for them to acknowledge my injury, because it might suggest some failure on their part to protect me from harm, some lack of vision. But I can barely imagine my own feelings of guilt if my son were laid out on the operating table with an angry doctor running stitches through his flesh. I don't know if I'd be able to talk about it either.

I suspect it was enough for them to see the gash in my face, enough of a jolt to jump-start that idling engine of parental guilt and crank it into overdrive. My dad and mom didn't need to be lectured, and I wish now that I could will my past self up and off that operating table into the pose of a confident and intelligent four-year-old child, a boy not stupefied by anesthesia, and deliver a rousing defense of my parents, a stirring oration praising their parenting and condemning the doctor for her insensitivity. I wish *that* boy could say something important about risk and the seduction of danger, about love and letting go. But his face is covered with blue paper and that's not his job. Not yet.

Pogo Stick Jumping.

The greatest number of jumps achieved is 105,338 by Michael Barban in 18 hours on September 12, 1978, in Florissant, Missouri.

Scott Spencer, 13, of Wilmington, Delaware, covered 6 miles in 6 1/2 hours in September, 1974. (1980, 477)

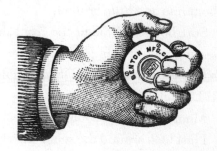

Tongues, Speaking In.

In elementary school Matt and I ride the bus with the other kids in the neighborhood. As his older, bigger brother, I guess I'm supposed to watch out for him and be his protector or something, but he doesn't seem like he needs much watching. In fact his independence is part of what annoys me so much about him as a *little* brother.

So I bounce through the front door as on any other day, wearing my royal blue Bruce Jenner tennis shoes (the ones that come with a replica Olympic gold medal) and carrying my NFL lunch box.

Mom smiles, greets me, and asks, "Where's your brother?"

I just look around the room and shrug my shoulders.

"Was he on the bus with you?"

"Yeah, I think so."

"Well, where is he now?"

"I don't know."

I look behind me, as if he'll be hiding back there. *Nothing.*

Panic sets in. I can see it in Mom's agitated hands. They flutter around her face like frightened birds. I realize then that I should be more worried.

"Did he get off at another stop?"

"I don't know."

"Are you sure he was on the bus?"

"I think so," I say, but I don't really know where he is or what happened.

Frantic phone calls are made to friends, parents, teachers, the principal, and the bus company. I'm not really too worried, but Mom holds the phone in her lap and bites her lip while they search. Mom has a lot of fear. Slowly, she's teaching me to own mine. It's not a bad thing, really—just the development of an active imagination.

The phone rings. Nobody has seen Matt. They're pretty sure he boarded the bus after school. When the driver is located again, she has already dropped all the kids off and parked her bus in the lot.

"Are you sure he's not on the bus?" Mom asks, and there's a pause. "Can you please just check again?" she asks. "Please."

We wait for what seems like hours, my mother and me at home, my father at work. We all start to imagine the worst. We can't help it. So we try to push the images out of our heads. Mom is crying. I don't want Matt to be gone. Not really. Not anymore. I just want him to walk through the door again.

The phone rings. It's the bus company.

They've found Matt sleeping in the bus, curled up beneath one of the green vinyl seats in the back. He's small enough that he fits perfectly under there.

"Oh, God. Thank you, thank you," Mom says. She hangs up and calls Dad. It is well after dark when he picks Matt up at the bus barn.

This was scary stuff for everyone involved, but Matt is not sitting in an office whimpering into his fist. He does not run screaming into Dad's arms, as I'm sure I would have. He is playing cards with some of the bus drivers and mechanics, four or five of these guys and my brother sitting around a table in the garage like old friends. When Dad comes to take him home, he doesn't want to leave. He's made some new friends.

Matt just isn't afraid of the things most people are afraid of. He plays by different rules.

. . .

I remember watching him bounce something like 850 times on a pogo stick in the driveway. We were always doing something noisy. We'd built bike jumps in the yard and carved out a dirt path in the grass with our motorcycles. I'm sure the neighbors hated us. We just didn't fit.

I was probably stomping around the driveway on some homemade stilts or stuffing Black Cat firecrackers into rotten apples when Matt mounted that squeaky old pogo stick. If anyone could set a Guinness Record in our family, Matt could. He had that unwavering focus and determination, a mix of obsessive and compulsive tendencies, which seems to define many record holders.

"You'll never break the record," I said. "It's like a hundred thousand jumps and eighteen hours."

"I can do it," he said as he sprang around the driveway.

"Yeah, right."

"Watch me."

I counted two hundred hops, and I have to admit that I was impressed. I'd messed around on the pogo stick too, even trying to see how far I could go, but it just wasn't fulfilling. I felt no sense of accomplishment, no real disappointment when I quit hopping and moved onto something else.

I'm also not sure I really wanted to break—or even attempt to break—a Guinness Record like Michael Barban's. I mean, you should see his face in the picture. He's just a mop-haired midwestern kid like us, and he looks so happy. I can't help but think he needs this record a lot more than Matt does, and as Matt came bouncing past me, counting out loud, I had the sudden urge to knock the shit out of my brother and send him sprawling into the flower beds.

Instead I just turned around and walked inside the house, convinced that without an audience to either entertain or annoy, he'd just quit bouncing.

I came back out a while later, and Matt was still going. I saw

him bouncing in and out of the garage, over cracks in the driveway. *Up and down, up and down, up and down.* At first he didn't notice me, he was so lost. He was in this pogo daze, and I watched him go. When he finally did see me, he just sort of grinned sheepishly and said, "four hundred twenty-five, four hundred twenty-six, four hundred twenty-seven."

Matt kept it going for some time, but nothing like Michael Barban or Scott Spencer, nothing close to eighteen hours or six miles. I guess he didn't have what it takes after all, didn't have the commitment. Still, he did teach me something about the motivations of some Guinness Record holders. For a lot of them, there's no real reason for their actions, no easy explanation.

If I had asked Matt why he kept going on that pogo stick, he would have said, "I don't know. It was fun." There's something intrinsically good or therapeutic or calming in the actions themselves that these people find gratifying, something independent of reward and recognition.

Yet it's hard for me to imagine doing anything consciously for eighteen hours. Swimming? Biking? Showering? Typing? And this is when the question pops up again. Why? What is his motivation? Maybe Michael was bouncing away from something like so many other kids our age trying to survive the seventies and eighties. It could've been something at home, some ugliness in his house. Maybe he never fit in right with the other children. Or it could just have been the rhythm of the bounce, that hypnotic *squish-pop* of the pogo, the slight squeak that develops after a few hours, chirping like a squirrel monkey. It could be he wanted to be a hero too and escape his humdrum life as a normal boy.

• • •

Matt speaks in tongues. Sort of. It's a game he plays when we're riding the bus or in the car with Dad. I'll point to a billboard or a street sign, and Matt will say the words backwards. He can do it almost instantly. *Burger King* becomes *Gnik Regrub*. Matt swaps *One Way* for *Yaw Eno*. *Holiday Inn* switches to *Nni Yadiloh* and sounds like some kind of beautiful Navajo word uttered only in sacred ceremonies.

He can break down words into letters and rearrange them in his head as if he were tossing Scrabble tiles around. The whole family will get into the game sometimes, trying to stump him, but it's creepy what he can do with words.

I still get snagged on the power of individual words, wrapped up in their own unique personalities. I can't bend and twist them like Matt does. It's almost as if they are mathematical equations that he simply picks apart for his own purposes. To me it seems almost blasphemous what he does to words. His skill unnerves me because it suggests a disregard for authority, an elevation of himself above the rules of language. Maybe I'm just jealous. Maybe it's just another time when Matt steps over a line that I'm waiting at with everyone else.

Knife.

The penknife with the greatest number of blades is the Year
Knife made by the cutlers Joseph Rodgers & Sons Ltd, of
Sheffield, England, whose trademark was granted in 1682.
The knife was built in 1822 with 1,822 blades, and was
designed to match the year of the Christian era until 2000 AD,
but had to halt at 1,973 because there was
no more space for blades. Now a way
has been found to add blades to 2,000.
(1982, 370)

Knives, Sharpest.

Dad gave me my first knife in my fifth year—a tiny folding jack-knife with a blue plastic handle and one thin blade. I loved that thing with all my heart. My granddad always carried a pock-etknife, my father too; so it was a rite of passage of sorts, and one I was happy to embrace.

I must have looked like a strange little kid with my hand shoved in my pocket much of the time, wrapped tight around the little knife, feeling the plastic ridges of the body and the metal curve of the folded blade. In my spare time, I whittled sticks into sharp points and carved my initials into pieces of scrap wood in the garage.

Things with my knife went fine for a while. The trouble started with a simple game of tag. Ronnie Olson, my best friend, this blond-haired, blue-eyed, all-star kid, had me cornered on a neighbor's deck and was taunting me, backing me into a corner, menacing me with his outstretched hands.

It was just a game, but fear welled up in my chest like water backing up in a sink drain. I looked down at the grass below and considered jumping, trying to gauge the distance. Ronnie moved closer, teasing me, threatening me. Without really thinking, I pulled out my jackknife, opened the blade, and waved it in the air, jabbing it at Ronnie.

"Come on," I said. "Try it."

Ronnie stopped dead in his tracks, and his chin dropped.

His eyes went wide. He pointed at my knife, turned, and ran straight down the deck stairs and across the yard, around the house to my front door, crying and blabbing to my mother.

I don't think Mom really knew what to say to me. I knew I had hurt her, scared her even. I doubt she'd wanted me to have the knife in the first place, but I'm sure she also knew how much I loved it. And she knew how close Ronnie and I were—really and truly best friends. It was hard to explain. I had no good reasons for my actions. I felt like I was on the verge of becoming someone other people referred to as a "bad kid" or "troubled."

When Dad came home, he talked with Mom for a while and then came up to my room and sat down on the edge of my bed. I was crying. He put his hand on my back and asked me to tell him what had happened. I tried to explain, and he listened. He was patient and caring. He didn't yell and scream or spank me or anything. He just listened to what I had to say. We talked about the apologies I'd have to make, and then he paused for a second. I knew what was coming.

He'd take my knife for sure—my beautiful, precious knife.

"There's got to be something else, something between us," he said.

"What?" I asked, knowing what he would say.

He paused. "I'm going to let you make that decision. You tell me what your punishment should be."

I looked at him. "Really? But what should I do?" I was stumped. I'd never been faced with this kind of decision.

"I guess that's up to you," he said. "I'll give you a minute to think about it." He stood up and stepped out into the hall. I heard the bathroom door close and the toilet seat smack against the tank. I sat there in my room, heavy with guilt, completely saturated, and somehow knew what I had to do. It just kind of came to me, the idea surfacing from somewhere deep inside.

The toilet flushed and Dad stepped back into my room. "Well," he said. "What's the word?"

I sat up on the edge of the bed. "I think I should have to throw my knife into Clinton Lake."

Dad was silent for a moment or two. He lowered his head and seemed to be trying to collect himself. He rubbed his fingers into his eyes.

"All right," he said, "that's it then." He left my room too choked up to say good night. I just buried my head in my pillow again.

A few days later we drove out to the lake and parked on the dam. We walked out onto the giant concrete spillway platform and stood there bawling our eyes out, the both of us. Dad and me. Father and son. Both of us guilty, Dad for giving me the knife in the first place, and me for ignoring his lessons and threatening my best friend.

Dad wrapped his big sea-monster hands around me and lifted me up over the railing. I reached a hand into my pocket, pulled it out, cocked my arm back as far as it would go, and tossed the knife. It fluttered through the air and barely made a noise as it disappeared into the rolling brown waters. We stumbled back to the car, Dad's arm draped over my shoulder.

Still today I can't drive over that dam, see that lake, without thinking about that moment. My father trusted me to inflict my own punishment, demanded that a five-year-old boy decide an appropriate sentence for pulling a knife on his best friend;

and it meant the world to me. No spanking I ever received, no mouth-washing with soap, no banishment to the elementary school hallways resonated through my personality like that moment. At the age of five, I had decided that I needed a dramatic, symbolic gesture to prove that I could be a good person, that I was not the kind of boy who pulls a knife on his best friend.

• • •

My father tells a story of when he was a boy and stabbed himself in the leg with *his* favorite pocketknife. He was carving something off a seat in an old car for reasons that remain unclear. He was cutting toward himself—the cardinal sin of all knife use—when the knife slipped and jammed into the side of his upper thigh.

When the small-town doctor saw what Dad had done, he pulled a long cotton swab from a jar on the counter, dipped it in rubbing alcohol, and without anesthetic, poked the swab into the hole in Dad's leg and swirled it around, scrubbing out the wound. He told Dad that this "ought to teach you a lesson about cutting toward yourself," and I'm sure the sting lingered for a while, but apparently not long enough.

I must have been about nine or ten when it happened again. Dad was our Cub Scout leader, and with his help, our den had designed a wooden footbridge that we planned to use for an initiation ceremony into the Webelo scouts. It was late at night. Everyone else was asleep. Dad was in the basement working on something for the bridge, and he was cutting toward himself again when the knife slipped off the table and plunged into his thigh, sticking in the bone. Asleep in the next room, I was awakened by Dad's cursing and screaming. But then the noise stopped, I heard him climb the stairs, and I went back to sleep.

Dad never did go to the hospital for that one, and it was a bad one too. He told me later how he'd sat down on the toilet that night with Mom in front of him trying to inspect the damage. He pulled the towel off the wound, bent his leg, and sprayed a stream of blood down the front of Mom's nightgown, sending her straight out of the bathroom and into a change of clothes. It took weeks for that thing to heal. It was deep, and the wound kept breaking open. He walked around stiff-legged and winced if anything touched his leg. Despite his assurances that it wasn't a big deal, I knew if I ever jammed a knife in my leg, I'd find my way to the hospital.

• • •

Around the same time I pulled a knife on my best friend, my father installed burglar alarms throughout the house. This was the seventies, and there wasn't a lot of crime in our neighborhood. I didn't really understand it at the time, but I learned later that an employee Dad had fired, a Vietnam veteran, had stormed into his office with a loaded M16 assault rifle and threatened to kill Dad and all of his partners.

I can understand how this might make you a bit overprotective as a parent. I can understand now how it might make you carry a .9 mm pistol under the seat of your truck and wire the whole house for safety. We had motion sensors and window alarms. We were ready. For what? I could only imagine. They never told me a thing. For my dad, though, there was a face to his fear, a reason to look over his shoulder.

It's strange the twists that life takes sometimes. Some fifteen years later, this same man would land a job at a local high
school as an assistant athletic trainer. He started working
there when I played basketball, and when an errant elbow had
split my eye open during a game, he had been the one to dab
the blood from my face with a towel and close the cut with a
butterfly bandage. His hands—the same hands that had held
an M16 rifle and pointed it at my father—worked tenderly
over my face. Dad watched the whole thing from the stands,
and I can't even imagine what he must have been thinking.

· · ·

There is another story I know only bits and pieces of, a story
tied to an ugly time in the history of my hometown. This was
before I was born. Mom was working as a teacher at West Junior High, the same school I would later attend. Dad worked
as a real estate broker, I think, or some kind of property man-
ager. He had an office near downtown in an ugly, nondescript
building.

The whole town was roiling with tension. There had been
murders, possibly racially motivated, and riots. The Memorial
Union on campus had been firebombed and burnt to a husk
of blackened brick. At one point martial law was imposed and
National Guardsmen were posted throughout the town. My
parents were never political types, not activists by any means,
but that didn't mean they weren't troubled by what they saw
around them. Dad had barely missed being drafted for Vietnam, and he used to talk about seeing boys with machine
guns standing on street corners, and feeling like he lived in a
war zone.

Dad's office was firebombed one night. Someone heaved a Molotov cocktail through his second-floor window, and it landed under his desk. The damage—both physical and psychological—was always minimized for me. I never got any details. The building still stands today. "No big deal," Dad would say. "Just a random thing."

I wanted to believe him, but part of me kept that nugget of a story, that whiff of something more sinister, and held it like a pearl, cherishing the mystery of the whole thing. Perhaps he had been targeted intentionally. Perhaps they considered him a symbol of something sinister—like corporate greed or development or bourgeois politics. I don't know, and I'm not sure if he does either. But it still helps sometimes to think danger isn't so random.

• • •

I was the only one who ever set off the alarms in our house. An early riser as a child, up often before anyone else but Mom, I used to wander the house looking for her. She was usually jogging with friends or working at Plymouth Church, taking those few moments that you need to survive as a parent.

As a kid I believed whatever my parents told me about the world. I hadn't developed any real skepticism or cynicism. I didn't know anything about Vietnam or war or anything like that. I didn't know about the threats Dad had faced. He practically forbade pessimism, insisting with zealot-like authority that everyone be happy—or at least act happy—and his philosophy made sense given the kind of world we were growing up in. We were pretty good at the whole happiness thing. But when I wandered alone in the house those early mornings, before the sun came up and *Super Friends* started at 7:00 A.M., I sniffed this lingering scent of something buried beneath the surface—secrets never shared, fear never recognized, or loss never acknowledged.

At the time I didn't know why, but inevitably my morning walks ended with me standing at the door, my hand on the knob, knowing that I'd set off the screeching alarm but still unable to resist opening it. I wonder now if I knew something intuitively about our family or the world and I just wanted the house to scream about it if nobody else would. You should have seen the way everyone jumped when I set off the alarm. Suddenly I didn't feel so lonely in the mornings.

• • •

When I was growing up in Lawrence in the seventies and early eighties, the closest thing we had to a Wal-Mart was Gibson's Discount Center. We spent a lot of time at Gibson's it seemed, buying camping equipment or toys or auto parts. They had everything. For a while we collected the Funk & Wagnalls encyclopedias they sold for ninety-nine cents per volume, but we made it only a few books in before we quit. Gibson's always put the seasonal and special offer displays at the front of the store, on the end of every aisle. They were often Corning Ware or old Halloween candy or cases of soda pop and those encyclopedias.

Once when we were there with Dad they had a display of kitchen knives tacked to a board and laid out in fan patterns. The display knives were all sheathed in blocks of Styrofoam, each with an identical black plastic handle. Dad, Matt, and I were all pulling knives out and inspecting them, running our thumbs crossways over the blades to check for sharpness. It was a kind of game since you couldn't tell from the handle or the Styrofoam how big the knife was until you pulled it out. Matt and I were comparing butcher knives when Dad tapped me on the shoulder.

"Look at this one," he said as he yanked the handle out of the Styrofoam and thrust the knife into my stomach.

I screamed at the top of my lungs and looked up at my father. People stared. Matt gasped. But it wasn't a knife after all, just a knife *sharpener*—long, round, dull, and harmless.

"Oh, God," Dad said. "I'm sorry. I'm so sorry. It was just a joke."

I wasn't really wounded, wasn't stabbed, but for a split second I thought my father had plunged a knife into my gut. But then he hadn't, it was a joke, and my heart was trying to dig its way out of my chest, and Matt was laughing, and the people weren't staring any longer, and we were just two boys shopping for knives with their father.

• • •

One other time we'd gone downtown with Dad to pick out a Christmas gift for Mom and stopped in a fancy kitchen store, a place that always smelled of cinnamon and coffee. Their shelves were piled with stainless steel pots and pans, expensive china, flatware, and lots of knives.

We'd been browsing the store, looking for something Mom might like, when Dad picked up a knife and fork meat-carving set that was part of a Japanese-style set of utensils. The knife slid into the handle of the fork so that together they formed a handsome black rectangle. Dad smiled at me.

"Hey, check it out," he said as I stepped toward him, "samurai meat cutter," and just as I reached out to grab the knife, he pulled it from its sheath in dramatic fashion and brandished the blade like a sword.

The blade split my thumb wide open, a deep cut that creased the pad for an inch or more. The knife was so sharp and the cut so clean that I barely felt it at first. Then the blood surged up into the wound, spilled out, and the pain came with it.

Without thinking I began to shake my thumb and screech, splattering blood all over the store as the ladies behind the counter gasped in horror and Dad tried to calm me down. He apologized profusely to everyone, but it wasn't really his fault. It wasn't anybody's fault, really. Just guy stuff. Just a mistake. Just a joke. But *Jesus* did it hurt and bleed a lot. The ladies scrambled around, frantically trying to find some paper towels, and I pressed them to the wound.

As we left the store, my thumb soaking the towels with blood, Dad said, "Raise the wound over your heart. It will slow the blood flow," and I thrust my hand into the air. I walked the whole way to the car like that. It took a long time to stop bleeding. We probably should've gone to the hospital, but we just drove home and bandaged up my thumb with some gauze and tape.

After plunging a couple of knives into his own body and suffering mightily for at least one of them at the hands of a doctor, Dad already had a well-developed distrust of the medical profession, and that may be why he didn't take me in for stitches. But now that I'm a father I understand something else about his actions. I've accidentally injured my own son. Several

69

times as a matter of fact. Once when he was just learning to walk and climbing around the patio outdoors, I gave him a boost but succeeded only in pushing him onto his face. He developed a blue bruise on the bridge of his nose that stayed for a few days. Another time we were playing on the bed and he smacked his forehead on the corner of the nightstand, punching a hole right into the skin that bled like hell.

Each time Malcolm got hurt I was racked with guilt and self-consciousness, almost to the point of panic. I wanted to pin a badge to his chest that said, "Hello, my Dad was just being a father and playing with me and I accidentally got hurt," so everyone would know. I didn't try to hurt him, but it happened. That's how it must have been for my dad. With all my wounds and sickness, he probably wanted to print up T-shirts with disclaimers explaining the scars and scabs. He'd already stood in that emergency room and heard them warn him of brain damage in his son, already stood there and listened to a doctor lecture him for being a bad father while she stitched up my face. I can't imagine he would've wanted to hear any of that again, and he didn't deserve to. These things happen. Children get wounded. They develop scar tissue. It gets easier.

Tree Eater.

If Joyce Kilmer were alive he would say: "I think that I shall never see / a man who eats a lovely tree" as Jay Gwaltney eats an 11-ft-tall birch sapling. He ate branches, leaves and the 4.7-in.-diameter trunk over a period of 89 hours to win $10,000 as first prize in a WKQX-Chicago radio station contest called "What's the Most Outrageous Thing You Would Do?" As he finished, he said, about the taste, "as far as trees go, it's not bad." (1982, 505)

Diet, Strangest.

The picture in my 1982 edition is black-and-white, so it's difficult to tell the full truth of this moment. But I suspect that young Jay Gwaltney wears a powder blue tuxedo, white shirt, and matching blue bow tie—something his mother helped him pick out from the JCPenney catalog.

I want to believe Jay was a lot like me. I see his yellow rose corsage, the bouquet of roses on the table. He is seated in a metal chair with vinyl padding. He's tall and broad-shouldered, maybe an oversize boy with obsessions and compulsions that set him apart from the other kids.

On the table sits a side plate with a saucer and spoon—maybe filled with some thin soup, a salty chicken or beef broth, something to wash down the wood. There is a coffee cup and a large, empty dinner plate. Jay's blond hair shines in the camera flash. A banner hangs behind him on the wall, the only visible word, "Chicago."

In his right hand he holds a sprig of birch sprouting seven or eight leaves. With his left hand he pulls at one of the leaf stems. He is ready. He does not look at the camera. He has made his decision. He stares down at his hands, eyeing the last remnant of his eleven-foot dinner sapling, perhaps wondering if it is worth the ten thousand dollars. It must have taken some time, some real commitment. He couldn't have done it all at this table in the picture, not wearing that pretty powder blue suit the whole time.

• • •

I imagine Jay's commitment, his own obsession. He's in the garage of his parents' home using Dad's power tools to grind the sapling down to sawdust. He sees a new image of himself reflected in the eyes of others, a heroic image, and he doesn't care about what they might whisper.

He's shoveling handfuls of birch shavings into his mouth, washing them down with buttermilk. His mother bakes sawdust pies with graham-cracker crusts. She mixes sawdust into milk shakes. She makes salads from the leaves and drenches them in dressing. His father cheers him on from the sofa. They'll do anything for their baby boy, anything to help him succeed, anything to get him out of the basement, and I'd bet Jay is dreaming of a Camaro or a catamaran, a ski trip to Aspen, a motorcycle, or a camper truck with a propane heater.

I doubt that he, like his mother, is dreaming of college or investments in the stock market. But it could be more than the ten thousand dollars. Maybe he knew Guinness was watching all along. Maybe he knew I was watching. I suspect Jay understood the immortality of the page, the legacy of living in a book so full of heroes and freaks. He could've been a lot like me, a misfit boy striving for identity in strange ways. Or maybe he just liked the taste of wood.

• • •

If I could find Jay Gwaltney today, I'd ask why he chose the birch tree. Was it the paper-like quality of the bark, the soft

wood? Did his Norwegian grandfather tell him stories of the
Old Country and how they used to drink birch tea? Did he
consider soft pine or ruddy dogwood, hard oak or red maple
with its fire leaves?

I'd ask him if he loved the Guinness Books too, if he'd seen
the pictures of Shridhar Chillal and Michael Barban, maybe
Benny and Billy McCrary. I'd ask how he made the step that
I couldn't—from voyeur to participant, from off-the-page to
on-the-page. How did he turn chance into choice? I'd like to
see the moment he heard about the contest on the radio, that
DJ's voice surfacing from the noise, and how it came to Jay as
if it were a voice from God. I wonder what made him think that
he could eat a tree, an eleven-foot tree, and that this would be
enough for the rest of his life.

I think a Guinness World Record would be enough for me. I
think I'd be proud of my accomplishments if I were Jay Gwaltney. But perhaps he never chose this path. Perhaps it was some
emptiness inside he was trying to fill. Perhaps he graduated
to eating forty-foot trees, redwoods, railroad ties, or untreated
telephone poles. Perhaps eating wood pulp was all he knew,
the only fulfillment he had.

Jay might have spent his prize money on a bungalow in the
old part of town, where the cottonwoods towered overhead,
and bought a wood-chipper right off the bat. When he worked
in the yard, he might've put a pinch of sawdust between his
cheek and gum.

He'd never fit into the neighborhood—no matter how hard
he tried—standing out there in his Carhartt overalls and his
safety goggles, feeding everything into that damn wood chipper. He'd frighten the children and old ladies who stopped to

watch, because now Jay's yard must be naked and brown, emptied of green and punctuated with stumps. He has worried the trees down to nothing. The neighbors point at annual rings, the shadow arcs of lost time, lost history.

He has planted a new grove of birch, and he says he's trying to cut back, but they are still angry about neighborhood character and the loss of shade. They're angry because their own children have begun to eat strange things too—twigs and paper, nuts and washers, entire boxes of Hot Tamales cinnamon candy, and several number-2 pencils. They're angry because Jay has a way of getting under your skin. Shridhar Chillal too. Michael Barban, Benny, Billy, and the others. He just follows different rules, different rhythms than everyone else.

If Jay Gwaltney were my neighbor, I'd join him for a pinch of sawdust on his porch. I might ask him to autograph my Guinness Book. I might ask him about commitment and obsession. I'd let him hold my son on his lap, and we could just sit and talk about nothing at all. I might do anything I could to help him fit in with the normal neighbors.

Biggest Bag.

The largest animal ever shot by any big game hunter was a bull African elephant *(Loxodonta africana africana)* shot by E. M. Nielsen of Columbus, Nebraska, 25 miles north-northeast of Mucusso, Angola, on November 7, 1974. The animal, brought down by a Westley Richards 0.425, stood 13 feet 8 inches at the shoulder. The greatest recorded lifetime bag is 556,000 birds, including 241,000 pheasants, by the 2nd Marquess of Ripon (1852–1923) of England. He himself dropped dead on a grouse moor after shooting his 52nd bird on the morning of September 22, 1923. (1980, 624)

Guns, Youngest.

Matt and I started shooting rifles with Dad when we were just boys. Mostly it was harmless target shooting. We'd drive out into the country and plunk cans and bottles with our rifles, maybe the occasional fluorescent light tube, poker chip, or pumpkin. Just kid stuff. Nothing too dangerous.

The first living thing I ever killed was a mangy jackrabbit. It was no trophy kill. I was eight years old and out prowling the farm roads in Western Kansas with my granddad. We were taking potshots at prairie dogs, never hitting anything, when he pulled the truck over to the side of the road, pointed at the jackrabbit hopping along in the brush, and told me to shoot it. I raised the .22 rifle up and out the window, sighting down the barrel. The first shot caught the rabbit in the hip and sent it leaping and gyrating in the brush, bouncing around frantically.

"Shoot him again," Granddad said. "Quick."

My second shot pegged him in the skull—easily the best shot I ever made. We got out of the truck and stood over the fresh kill. The rabbit just seemed to melt into the landscape.

"What now?" I asked.

"Leave him," my grandfather said. "Coyotes will take it." We climbed back into the truck and kept on driving, our tires cooking up great clouds of dust that spilled over the prairie.

I was eight years old and I had become a killer.

"They're pests," my granddad had said. "They destroy crops. Besides, that one was sickly, probably dying anyway."

That night I dreamed of killing a white, fluffy bunny, the cute kind you see in pet stores, with their floppy ears and wriggly noses. I called home the next day and cried to my mother over the phone.

Granddad tried to help by telling me that not only was I doing that farmer a favor but the jackrabbit would have died a painful death of starvation anyway. I was putting it out of its misery. I did a good thing, a merciful thing. Somehow I understood then that one small part of being a boy in our family was learning how to kill small, defenseless animals and live with it.

• • •

One night, we came home from a family outing to the sound of high-pitched screaming. The noise was stretched in anguish and ringing through the neighborhood. It seemed to be coming from the backyard. The dog was barking incessantly, and Dad knew right away what it was.

"That's a rabbit," he said as we pulled into the driveway. He'd heard the sound before. But for the rest of us it was a new and horrifying assault on the senses, a persistent squealing— almost like the burglar alarms I had set off regularly in our old house, or a wailing infant.

The jackrabbit I killed didn't scream like this. He only jumped and jerked around awkwardly, looking more surprised than anything, and barely made a noise. But this rabbit was different. This rabbit was letting us know about his pain, and I just wanted him to shut up about it. Mom, Matt, and I each clamped our hands over our ears. I thought about the jackrabbit roundups Dad had witnessed as a boy and how the air must have been filled with this sound as they killed hundreds, even thousands of jackrabbits and burned them in piles.

Dad parked the car in the garage, and we waited inside the house while he slipped out the back door and investigated. He came back, herding the dog in front of him, and headed straight for the gun cabinet in the basement.

"It's a rabbit all right," he said as he clomped down the stairs. His voice came up from the basement. "Got stuck in the fence and Skipper did a number on him."

The cottontail had tried to jump through the chain-link but got his hind legs stuck in the mesh. Our dog, Skipper, a tough-nosed fox terrier, had shredded the rabbit's hindquarters, nearly eating the thing alive. Her snout was matted with blood, and as I tried to keep her back, she skittered around on the tile in the laundry room, whimpering and yipping. She was just operating on instinct. Dad loaded his .22 caliber Marlin rifle, and I waited inside, holding the dog back with my foot, as he went out again.

I watched out the window as Dad moved quickly across the grass and disappeared into the trees and shrubs along the back fence. The rabbit screamed and screamed until one quick *pop* of the rifle ended it, barely a sound at all, and the ordeal was over. Dad pulled the rabbit back through the fence and dropped the body in the trash can.

• • •

For some reason it always takes me two shots to kill a rabbit. I'm following a covey of quail down the grassy banks of a long-dry streambed in Western Kansas. Matt and I are working these birds together, pushing them up the creek, hoping to flush them out in the open, where we can get a shot.

Matt doesn't really like hunting for quail. "It's too much work for too little shooting," he says. He's impatient. But I like walking around and tracking birds and just being outside. It feels like you're really hunting.

It's a known fact that quail will run on the ground as long as they can, even hide in the brush until you nearly step on them, then burst up in a mad flapping and cooing—often scaring the living shit out of you. If you get a shot, it's typically not very clean, and the bird may still be alive when you find it. If so, you'll need to pinch the head between your thumb and forefinger and then twist until the head comes off. This leaves a small, pink, fleshy stump of a neck, and sometimes the wings will beat for a few seconds afterward. A heart shot is the most bizarre thing. At first you think you've missed because the bird will keep flying for a few seconds, its nerves and muscles still working, and then it just drops like a stone.

So Matt and I are kicking through some high grass when I step on a hollow log and it's not a quail I frighten but a cottontail rabbit that comes scampering out the end. Without thinking I raise my twelve-gauge, swing the barrel, and fire, sending the rabbit head over heels. It's instinct that makes me fire, no thought at all, just reaction.

The amber-eyed rabbit twitches in the grass when I approach, gun raised, to finish the job, and I swear it looks at me, stares right in my eyes. I have no answer really, no justification. I won't be eating this rabbit. I raise the gun and fire again, filling the body with buckshot, watching the muscles go loose and just sort of deflate. I feel like I should do something, but there isn't anything to be done. So I just leave it there and keep walking, looking for birds, hoping a coyote will find the carcass. The killing part came more easily this time, but dealing with it is just as bad.

• • •

At the age of ten I was a card-carrying junior member of the NRA. I fired guns at targets in the basement of a building on campus, passed some safety tests, paid dues, and joined the ranks. In Mrs. Carter's class we were asked to draw logos for ourselves, personal symbols, and mine consisted of two crossed rifles and crude drawings of a motorcycle, a book, and a knife. Cute, huh?

Combined with my (perhaps unhealthy) obsession with Abe Lincoln's violent demise (I could recite a minute-by-minute time line of the day he was assassinated), this would probably be enough today to get me expelled from school and placed in some kind of group home or alternative school. But in the early eighties it wasn't so abnormal. Or maybe it was abnormal and I just didn't realize it. It did seem they were always trying to get me to talk to the school counselor. She was nice. We'd go driving in her car to get ice cream or something, and she would ask if I had angry or violent thoughts.

Of course I did. I was a boy. But I'd try to convince her that I was fine and that she had nothing to worry about. It seemed like everyone was telling me I needed to talk about my feelings. But they didn't get it. I didn't really have feelings—at least not ones I could recognize. And besides, I had my journal to express myself freely.

Or at least I thought I did.

Mrs. Carter had asked us to keep a journal every day, something private that we didn't have to share with anyone. She promised us she would only check to see that we were writing and she wouldn't read the entries. But she lied. She read something critical I wrote about her class. I don't remember what it was, but she called me out in front of the other kids, making me feel so small and stupid, so violated.

It was a mistake she would soon regret, as I launched into daily journal tirades against her, accusing her of Nazi surveillance tactics and comparing her to Hitler. You see, there was nothing she could do about it since she was still telling the other children that she didn't read their journals. Eventually she just stopped collecting them.

It was a little disturbing how much I enjoyed using words against her—and obviously a bit unfair and manipulative on my part. She kind of *had* to read what we were writing. That was her job. But every day I could see her shrivel from me, afraid to confront me, afraid of the anger she had unleashed. Obviously trust was a big issue for me at that time. I couldn't blame her. It wasn't her fault. But the lesson I learned, oddly enough, was an early lesson on the power of words. I learned I could exercise some modicum of control over a world that had begun to seem decidedly out of control. With words I could seek vengeance. Not really a novel idea for disaffected writer types but one we all seem to learn nonetheless.

• • •

It's not something I like to admit, but I used to dream of becoming a sniper. Home alone, I'd occasionally point my little

.22 rifle out the window at cats and dogs, even cars. Sure, our gun cabinet had a key, but I always knew where Dad hid the key, so it was no problem getting in. There my curiosity was rewarded with my .22 rifle and other, forbidden, weapons— Dad's sawed-off shotgun and billy club, his beautiful lever-action Marlin rifle. I loved to work the pump action of his sawed-off shotgun—holding it loose against my side and then jerking it up, cramming the stock back and forth, and dry-firing it at the television.

In real life the gun only made a loud, metallic click when I pulled the trigger. In my imagination, it boomed and destroyed everything in sight. In my imagination the gun gave me power and sex appeal like Clint Eastwood, but I never would have taken it out of our house, into a public place, never would have actually used a gun against anyone.

That just wasn't a reality I was interested in exploring. Maybe Matt and I had killed enough small mammals and birds to know what guns can do. Maybe it was my father's insistent lessons in gun safety. We took classes. We learned to disassemble and clean every part of our own guns with military-like precision and care. We never owned BB guns because they were "toys" and "guns are not toys."

This sort of made sense to me. It was the same rationale Dad used to forbid us from owning *any* realistic toy guns. Even playing with our Star Wars replica weapons was tightly controlled. Dad wouldn't let us pretend to shoot each other. He told us that you never point a gun at something, "unless you plan to kill it." Matt and I would be running around the house, playing Star Wars or something, and he'd gesture at the barrel of my Han Solo laser pistol. "You plan to kill your brother?"

he'd ask, tracing the path of my swinging gun barrel as it crossed over Matt's heart.

• • •

When we moved out of the duplex and bought the house near campus, we were lucky to move into a neighborhood with lots of kids our age. We formed our own packs and herds, pairing off, tripling up for various misadventures. Our house was centrally located and often served as the playground.

We played a version of baseball we called "batball" that involved hitting a partially deflated volleyball with an aluminum bat and running the bases around our yard. There were football games on Saturday mornings and basketball games under the floodlights. We built bike jumps in the yard and launched ourselves into the air over and over again.

Once Ben Hobbs took flight on his bike, tilted in the air, and came down squarely on his right shoulder, breaking his collarbone. Several of us kids watched Ben take the jump, and we all knew when he hit the ground that something was wrong.

Darren Lewis pointed at Ben and cupped his hand to his mouth. "Oh God," he said.

Darren was a wiry kid who lived across the street from Ben and was known in the neighborhood for his Guinness-worthy eating abilities. He could eat more hot dogs than anyone and he never gained a pound. Matt was there and Joey Kemper too—all of us watching Ben writhe in pain in the yard, his bike wheels still spinning nearby. We gawked at the distorted shape of his shoulder, the bone poking up against the skin.

"Man, you broke something," Joey said. "Your shoulder is lumpy in all the wrong places."

"Ooo, that's bad," we all agreed.

Ben stood up, clutching his arm against his side, and ran home, leaving his bike in our yard.

Joey picked up the bike and rode after him. He was a short, funny kid with a thick shock of black hair and a bright smile. He was always smaller than the other kids were but made up for it with a big personality. He made everyone laugh. Joey was Matt's age, and he spent a lot of time with Ben and Darren. Matt and I kind of moved between their circle of friends at the west end of Stratford and others we'd made in different parts of the neighborhood.

I had started drifting apart from Ben and the other kids. Of course we all still saw one another at school, and Joey's mother worked with my dad. Joey had recently gone through his parents' divorce. Darren too. We were all just trying to survive, trying to fit in. We were just kids. That's all. Just kids.

That's why it was so hard to take when Ben, trying to show off for Joey and Darren, took a hunting rifle out of the closet, pointed it at Joey, and pulled the trigger.

Of course the rifle shouldn't have been loaded and the bullet shouldn't have passed through Joey's chest and lodged in the wall. But it happened, and Joey died almost instantly.

On some level Matt and I both recognized that it could have been either one of us in Ben's shoes, even Joey's shoes. Ben was a good kid, a fun guy who never meant anyone harm, and Joey was his best friend.

Ben seemed to just kind of fade into the background after that. I still think about him every time I read a news report about one child accidentally shooting another, and I think about how he was a victim too, not a criminal at all. He lost his best friend and his innocence. I wonder how anyone keeps living after something like that.

My father had to break the news to Joey's mother while she was at work, and later he had another long talk with us about gun safety. We never kept loaded guns in the house, but the bullets were always nearby, and I'm sure I'd shown off our guns to friends, maybe even held them and pulled the triggers, dry-firing just to hear the hammer hit the chamber. Dad had trained us well, drummed safety lessons into our heads, but you can't prepare for everything. You can't prevent a child's curiosity. You can't teach him to avoid danger entirely, or he'll never really live. You have to teach him how to survive.

Motorcycle Stunting.

The greatest endurance feat on a "wall of death" was 3 hours 4 minutes by the motorcyclist Louis W. "Speedy" Babbs (1908–1976) on a 32-foot-diameter silo, refueling in motion, at the Venice Amusement Pier, California, on October 11, 1929. In 1934, Babbs performed 1,003 consecutive loop-the-loops, sitting side-saddle in an 18-foot-diameter globe at Ocean Park Pier, California. In a life of stunting, Babbs, who proclaimed "Stuntmen are not fools," had broken 56 bones. (1980, 473)

Danger Boys, World's Greatest.

Dad's rusty-red Ford Gran Torino station wagon—a big and beefy family car—had a CB radio that looked like a telephone. His car was wired up to a switchboard at his office and a woman named Linda, who connected him to the world if he wanted. I told the other kids that he had a car phone.

Dad wore polyester shirts with big collars, Highway Patrol sunglasses, and these shaggy sideburns. His gigantic size and presence filled up spaces. In the car we ate from crisp plastic bags of fried pork skins and sipped from pony bottles of Miller beer. We sang along to "Elvira" by the Oak Ridge Boys or "Silver-Tongued Devil" by Kris Kristofferson.

Matt sat up front with Dad. I rode in the wide backseat—the orange vinyl rolled and glazed like a bread loaf—and I couldn't yet imagine that there was anything dangerous about two boys drinking beer with their father, listening to country music, and shooting guns on the weekends.

• • •

Dad's ears must have burned with Mom's worries. She knew about the beer and the pork skins and the guns and the motorcycles, but I'm not sure she knew the thrill we found dancing along the thin line between safety and danger, between right and wrong.

Sure it was probably "wrong" to feed alcohol and pork

by-products to a child, perhaps "dangerous" to put a gun in his hands or give him a motorcycle. But among friends—that's what we were to one another—these words didn't seem to carry much weight, especially when we had so much fun together. Besides, it's not like Dad got drunk and reckless. Mom knew whom she had married. He was rarely out of control, even when he acted dangerous.

Most times, Dad was responsible to a fault. Still, she'd also seen him push limits on family vacations, step ever so lightly across the line, carrying Matt and me with him. She had to wonder about the safety of her children. We'd stop the car at a roadside vista, the four of us standing at an iron railing, gazing out at some panoramic view of mountains. Dad would lift Matt and me up and hold each one of us out over the rails so we could look straight down at the rocks or river or highway below.

Every single time, he'd loosen his grip just slightly, just enough to give us the sensation of falling, and then clamp back down again with his giant hands. There was immortality in that instant of separation, a fearless, weightless feeling I could enjoy only because Dad's hands were there to pull me back. Matt, I imagine, lived his whole life for that instant, that moment of separation. He couldn't get enough.

• • •

Interstate 40 between Empire and Winter Park, Colorado, is made for danger. A ribbon of asphalt clings to the mountainside and drops sheer cliffs down to rocky slopes. My wife, Rachel, and I live just over the Front Range of the Rockies and often drive this road with our son, Malcolm, strapped into his car seat with the dog riding beside him. At least once a year, I hear a story about a rock tumbling off the mountainside and smashing into a car. Such a random thing. But I still can't help gazing up sometimes at the rocks above and wondering just how close we've come.

When I was a boy my family made the trip up from Kansas almost every summer. To us, sweltering in the flat, humid days of summer, Colorado seemed a promised land of elevation and air. Now I *live* in Colorado and don't get up into the mountains as often as I'd like. The drive up Berthoud Pass puts you out on the edge fast. There is no shoulder to speak of, nothing but space and gravity. I steer way clear of the edges, frightened at the vertigo I sometimes feel when looking down. But it's always worth the drive once we get there.

When we were kids, Dad liked to nudge the right front tire off the pavement, just a hair, to frighten us. Even though I knew it was coming, my heart still shuddered when I heard the gravel spitting up under the Ford and watched the car point off the edge, over the line, for just a split second.

Dad smiled and chuckled at the white-knuckled grips Mom and I clamped down on door handles. Matt sat there peaceful and serene, enjoying the thrill, even laughing a little, but I couldn't help imagining what it would feel like to go over—all four of us rattling around like pebbles in a can, hoping to slam into a tree just to stop the roll.

I could indulge in these imaginings as a child only because my father is an excellent driver, only because I trusted him completely. Matt always seemed incapable of imagining or unwilling to imagine his own death. This fearlessness is what allowed him to sit on the floor of our garage and pound .22 rifle shells with a hammer while I hovered over him stammering out warnings, pleading with him, describing the ricochet of bullets, holes in skulls, our father's wrath, our mother's tears. I wondered if he was doing it just to spite me, just to see the fear wash over me. Matt always claimed that this never happened, that I was lying just to make him seem foolish, but I know what I saw.

At the end of Berthoud Pass is the small ski town of Winter Park and the Fraser Valley. My family owns a cabin in the heart of Winter Park, and I still find myself there a few times a year. We like to strap our son in the backpack and stomp around the woods on snowshoes. It occurs to me that this may be the last year we'll be able to do that. Soon he won't tolerate being carried and will want to strike out on his own into the forest.

My family built this cabin in 1963, when there wasn't much happening in the valley. The ski resort was small and undeveloped. The cabin was intended to be a summer retreat. In fact they had bought the land because they had spent several summer weeks in the valley at a lodge called Miller's Inn. There are pictures on the wall of my dad, his two sisters, and his parents lined up in chairs in front of the old porch.

When Mr. Miller started selling off residential lots, my grandparents were the first to buy. With the help of one carpenter, my dad, my mom, my aunts and uncles all pitched in to build the cabin from the ground up. Today you can look in an album and see old photos of my mother and father. Taken during construction of the cabin, when they are still in college and have that fresh-faced look that Rachel and I shared during our school days, the photos offer possibility and promise.

My mom is strikingly beautiful, and Dad doesn't look bad himself. He's surprisingly thin and wiry, with those trademark sunken eyes. They remind me of images of myself in the early years of college, before I blew out my knee, when I too was thin and fit. I see a little bit of both Matt and me in their faces, even though we weren't in the picture yet. That's the thing about family photos. They seem to capture the present and contain the past but can't come close to predicting the future.

• • •

During a recent visit to my parents' house, I dug through a sagging box of old photographs and found a black-and-white of Matt and me sitting on a porch with a wooden Indian. On the back of the photo it says, "Dodge City, 1976."

For some reason, the wooden Indian's hand is placed so that it smothers my crotch. I don't really seem to mind. In fact I seem to like it. We sit on a clapboard porch, and I cling to his arm like a baby monkey. The man wears a stiff shirt, and his denim jeans shine like they've been varnished with polyurethane. He just sits there with his long, black braids, his beaded headband, and one feather rising up in the back. The corners of his mouth are pulled into a frown, his eyes rolled up to the sky. One foot tucked behind the other, he leans toward me.

He seems to need me as much as I need him.

His long, bony hand, black in the photo, cups my crotch, and his silver ring sparkles against my dark pants. Matt sits on the other side of him, holding the Indian's other hand delicately in his own—as if he is visiting the man for tea, sitting with him during the long hours of old age. Matt's white cowboy hat rests in his lap. Of course it's a white hat. He's the good brother. His short legs barely hang over the edge of the chair. He stares at me, not at the camera.

With my T-shirt tucked into a big leather belt, I mug my ugly smile for the camera. I have this one discolored tooth right up front in the middle. The nerve was killed when I fell on a brick at one of Dad's construction sites and the tooth just turned brown. My cheek scar should be there too, but it's hard to find.

Of course I am the brother in the black hat.

After this, we will ride—outlaw brothers looting barrels of rock candy, swinging cork pistols, and losing at high-stakes games of go fish or crazy eights. At the Boot Hill cemetery, we will stand over a grave marked with boots toed up through the soil and each of us will try to imagine what's connected to the feet. Are those the digits of a hanged man, blue with blood and swollen in their socks? We will imagine gun battles and dramatic deaths in the dusty streets. We will imagine our own trigger fingers but can't yet see how everything will change.

In the photo, Matt's are the only feet you can see, and this somehow makes him more real than anything. He's complete, captured for posterity. The Indian and I, the chairs, all seem to hover outside the edges of the frame. We barely exist the way Matt does. I remember this day. I don't remember tumbleweeds or the reflection of parents in a window, something that might make this more of a story. But what remains is not meaning, not some fixed image of brothers, but pure possibility. If we had been cowboy siblings in the Old West, I know we'd have made friends with this Indian. We might have been a crime-fighting trio.

He looks now like petrified wood, as if he was dug out of the desert, dusted off, and propped up on this porch. But he still could've been my friend, even in his wooden state. Matt and I would have had to share, and it would have been difficult. I'm sure we'd have had different ideas about what sort of care a wooden Indian needs. When it was my turn to watch him, he'd have sat in the corner of my room and scared away the fevers. I'd have painted and varnished him when he needed it. I'd have changed his clothes and taken him to school. We'd have been famous together. People would've said, "There goes that boy and his wooden Indian." And nobody would've whispered about the way he touches me still in this picture.

· · ·

I know Dad is the one who took that picture of Matt and me and the wooden Indian. He was always the photographer, the recorder and keeper of memories on our family vacations. He carried a big camera bag of film and a huge telephoto lens. At home he kept rolls of 16-millimeter film in those big metal cans. He always had shelves of books, shoe boxes full of old pictures, and trunks filled with mementos from his Boy Scout days.

I was fascinated with his books, and his "College" dictionary was one I especially loved to read. It seemed special, unique to an alien world, the world of "College." I had lurid fantasies about what "College" would be like, picturing all sorts of wild things—most of them based on the movie *Animal House* or on stories Dad told, which all pretty much sounded like *Animal House*. But this wasn't the only book of his that I secretly consulted. Somewhere nearby on the shelf, wedged between James Michener and Leon Uris, was *The Playboy Book of Limericks*—a thick yellow book that frequently beckoned me with clever, filthy rhymes about men from Rangoon and women from Nantucket. It was often more than I could resist.

One time Ronnie Olson and I sneaked into the playhouse Dad had built under the stairs and closed the door behind us. I pulled the string for the light, and the dim bulb flickered. We sat down cross-legged. I slid my fingers into the thick paper side of Dad's College dictionary and flopped it open in my lap, turning to the first dirty word I could think of. The book had the musty smell of old paper.

"Fuck," I whispered, pointing to the word, and we both giggled.

I lifted up a carpet scrap, and as I spelled out the word, Ronnie carefully transcribed it onto the floor of the playhouse with a blue Crayola.

We read the definition for *fuck* and had to look up other words, like *coitus*. We marched through our own lists of words, ones we had mostly learned from our fathers, looking up synonyms listed in the definitions, and soon the floor was covered with *shit, fuck, piss, pussy, penis, boob, tit,* and anything else we could think to look up.

Later I would sneak back in, lift up the carpet, and rub my fingers over the raised, waxy curse words, repeating them under my breath.

I wonder now if the people who purchased the house after we moved discovered our foul-fingered scribblings. It's not easy to clean crayon off of cement. They would have had to scrape away the wax with a putty knife or a chisel. So maybe

they just left it, carpeted over it, and those words are still down
there, hidden and dusty with age.

• • •

Matt and I convince Dad that we are old enough to see an
R-rated movie. We've grown tired of the 1969 *Playboy* issue
"Behind the Iron Curtain" Dad keeps barely hidden amid a
stack of other magazines in the basement. We've seen Brooke
Shields in *The Blue Lagoon*. We've watched Benny Hill's panty
fests on late-night TV, and we want more. We demand that
Dad take us to see *The Sorceress*, a Greek myth adventure saga
featuring half-naked blond twins on horseback who just happened to be endowed with powers of sorcery.

Dad takes us to the Sunday matinee. You would think that
two prepubescent boys couldn't have gotten enough of this,
and I wish that were the case. But the sad truth is I was horrified at the lack of plot, disgusted by all the rampant, pointless
fucking. I wanted some action scenes, fights, or anything besides the twins riding their horses in extremely slow motion,
their plastic-enhanced breasts bobbing and flopping in uni-
son. It was all rather traumatizing.

Now I can recognize this movie as B-quality soft-core porn
—a paper-thin plot that's really just an excuse for elaborate
costumes and choreographed sex. But as a boy I imagined that
all R-rated movies were like this one. There was horseback sex,
tent sex, river sex, and palace sex, lots of loose white robes and
gilded underpants. Lots of gods and goddesses behaving badly.
But how were we to know what it would be like? We were just
two curious boys with a permissive father.

We didn't last long, walked out of the theater before the

movie was half over. To this day I don't know what Dad was thinking. Did he somehow know it would be *that* bad, so bad his boys would actually walk out of a movie featuring topless twins on horseback? Or did he think we might actually learn something from the movie, some lesson about casual sex, Greek mythology, or sorcery? It's hard to say for sure, but I do know that it was a long time before Matt and I asked Dad to take us to another R-rated movie.

Strangely enough, there were times in our lives when both of our parents attempted to educate us with seminal works of film. With Mom we saw movies like *Amadeus, Gandhi,* and *Places in the Heart*—movies dealing with spirituality and heroism, art and passion. With Dad it was movies like *Cool Hand Luke, Deliverance, Bullitt, Serpico, Papillon,* and anything with Clint Eastwood or Charles Bronson. As I look back on these movies, the quick lessons I glean involve driving during kick-ass car chases, shooting during ass-kicking gun battles, dropping witty, sarcastic banter at the most opportune moments, exacting bloody, crowd-pleasing vengeance—all of this mixed in with some tips on how to survive in and/or escape from prison, and practical lessons on what to do if you're ever stalked in the woods by toothless, butt-raping hillbillies.

Clearly these are important lessons that every young boy should learn.

What I never told my dad is that I always had a bit of a crush on Paul Newman in *Cool Hand Luke.* I mean, I was just like George Kennedy—all gushy over Luke, that ol' egg-eating fool. Luke was a real hero—flawed and beautiful—and he made me want to use words like *dreamy* or *delicious.*

I can't help but wonder what sorts of movies I'll show my

own son, what sorts of lessons he'll glean from *Star Wars* and *The Warriors* (the coolest gang movie ever, by the way), or *The Terminator* and *Red Dawn*. I know his mother will be working on him with *Sixteen Candles, Pretty in Pink,* and *Desperately Seeking Susan.* There has to be some balance, right?

• • •

My father took 16-millimeter film footage of Matt and me playing in the creek behind the big house. It must have been just after a rainstorm, because the creek banks are muddy and the water a rich chocolate brown color. The creek is running high. We're shirtless and have the wiry bodies of boys who spend a lot of time outdoors. This is the same creek where we fished for crawdads and pulled leeches from our skin, the same creek that filled and flooded the golf course during big rains, giving the neighborhood a long, shallow lake dotted with green, manicured islands.

In the footage Dad shot, Matt and I climb the muddy creek bank and slide down, launching and landing with a splash. Again and again we scramble up the bank, our bellies pressed against the mud, and slide down. Feetfirst. Headfirst. Sideways. We crash into each other, dunk each other, and throw mud. It's our own private waterslide, our own mud pit of fun, and you can see our white smiles spread between muddy lips as we mug for Dad's camera.

As much fun as that day was, we probably had more fun watching the film years later. Dad would set up the projector and show the old movies on the living room wall. Along with the creek film, there's the footage of Matt and me playing in our diapers, spraying each other with hoses, and riding our Big Wheels around the cul-de-sac.

The highlight of the evening always came at the end, when Dad left the projector on and ran the film backward. Like so many things my father did, it seemed to alter the physics of reality. Matt and I leap from the depths of the creek like giant fish breaking the surface and then rocket up the bank on our bellies. Inexplicably, we walk backward down to the water and lower ourselves in slowly and carefully, as in some sort of voluntary baptism—only to be violently spewed up again and deposited on the bank a few seconds later. We look almost supernatural the way we seem to spawn from the muddy water, born again and again through images flickering on the living room wall.

• • •

Once, after the television quits working, Dad lets us tear it apart one piece at a time. This is one of those big wooden-cabinet televisions, a Zenith I think, and Dad figures he can salvage the cabinet for the new television he just bought. He gives us screwdrivers and pliers, several wrenches, wire cutters, and we open up the back of the thing.

Matt and I hunker down in front of the TV's guts, taking it one screw at a time, working our way through masses of wires, switchboards, and tubes. We're burrowing animals, digging our way into the television. Matt and I yank out fuses and circuits, speculating on their function.

"This one's the cartoon circuit," Matt says, holding up an insect-like fuse.

"I've got the sports chip," I say, waving a circuit board around.

"Oooo, it's the soap opera fuse," Matt says, pinching his nose and tossing it over his shoulder.

We dig and pull, twist and yank, until all that's left is the big, smoke gray screen and the wooden cabinet. The screen looks decidedly low-tech, like some sort of river stone or glassy root that sprouted and grew there. But we find the fasteners, remove them, and pull the smooth orb out, setting it on top of the cabinet. Later, when Mom is away, the three of us toss the screen in the back of the truck, drive out to one of our favorite spots, and plunk it full of bullet holes.

• • •

Dad has this way of making the most mundane activities seem adventurous. It could be salvaging a television cabinet or it could be a long family road trip from Kansas to Colorado. By the time we hit Denver, Matt and I would be buzzing with anticipation, squirming in our seats, just waiting to get to the cabin.

Several spots along I-40 between Denver and Winter Park are marked with yellow signs warning drivers to "Watch for Falling Rock." Every trip, Dad tells a story we've heard before, one we've come to expect but one we still beg to hear. You see, there was an Indian boy who wandered off from his parents and became lost in the Rocky Mountains. His father, a wise old chief crippled with sorrow, painted up these signs, asking our help in looking for his lost boy. That's why you see those yellow signs, "Watch for Falling Rock."

Dad doesn't have to remind us. Matt and I peel our eyes for

the signs. We gaze out the windows of our car into thick stands of lodgepole pines, scanning ridgelines, looking for a little lost Indian boy named Falling Rock wandering around in a loin-cloth. Maybe he carries a spear and walks with a pet squirrel on his shoulder. Maybe he can come live with us in Kansas and teach us how to skin a beaver. We never think to look for rocks falling from their perches, smashing through our car. This is the kind of fear that takes years to develop. We just want to help the boy get home safely, back to his father.

• • •

For me Winter Park is always about motorcycles. Now it bills itself the "Mountain Bike Capital of the World" and is often overrun in the summers with shiny spandex-clad bikers, but when I was a kid, it was often just Dad, Matt, and I out there in the woods on our noisy Yamahas.

At first Dad rode only with his friend Roger. We'd go to the cabin, and Roger would drive out and meet us there. He worked with Dad and owned the excavation side of their con-struction company. He and Dad would disappear on the bikes, sometimes for a day or two, leaving us back at the cabin with Mom. I don't think he ever intended to be so nuts about mo-torcycles. It just sort of happened.

Dad bought his first motorcycle during the energy crisis in the eighties. It was a little green Yamaha 100 cc—basically an oversize moped. He weighed somewhere around 260 pounds and wore a bulbous blue helmet, looking like a circus act put-tering up the street. To save money on gasoline, he rode that motorcycle every day to work, where he built large subdivi-sions of new homes and managed every phase of the construction process, from foundation to finish, sales, rental, and even security.

The energy crisis was tough on his business, though. He designed and built the house where we lived, but in the summers we slept in the cool basement so as not to run the air conditioner. Matt and I shared a room. Dad and Mom were at the end of the hall. I think driving the motorcycle made Dad feel like he had some control over the oil crisis, some choice in the matter.

His energy-saving efforts turned out to be a good practice. We traded our massive Ford station wagon and sedan in for a gold Corolla wagon for Mom and the 1980 blue Toyota pickup that would become the vehicle for so many of our adventures.

Dad bought that motorcycle and that little, fuel-efficient Japanese truck and started building solar homes too. He was trying to adapt, trying to make it work. Sometimes Matt and I would help him run electrical conduit in the homes after the framers had finished and before the finish carpenters, plumbers, and painters started. We'd climb up in the attic and scamper from joist to joist, stringing the wire with us and pushing it into outlet boxes. Dad would stand below and give us directions. We loved every minute of it. Those houses were like big wooden jungle gyms. I still love to walk through a house in progress and try to imagine how everything will take shape. The physics and art of construction amazes me. It's easy to take something like a staircase for granted, but not if you've seen one being built.

Dad worked for a while in Bartlesville, Oklahoma, building an assisted-living retirement community, a rather massive project called Green Country Village. He tells a story about a time

Matt visited during the construction process and helped Dad run conduit through the rafters. This was a little different than his energy-efficient solar homes of the eighties. These ceiling joists were three times as big, farther apart and forty feet off the ground. Matt climbed up there and jumped from joist to joist, dancing his way across the central atrium like some kind of trapeze artist while Dad watched from below. One slip and he would have fallen four stories down to concrete. Dad tells the story with a mix of awe, guilt, fear, and pride. There's an understanding between us that Matt is different, fearless in a way we never will be. He's a danger boy in a league of his own.

• • •

Dad's always said Matt was better on wheels than either one of us. The implication here for me is that Matt has always seemed better at living and more comfortable in his body. Dad said it's because Matt never thought about what he was doing. He just relaxed and rode out the bumps. He followed the spirit of my father's lessons. To Matt, crashing was something you allowed, even created, and not something that simply *happened*. He never crashed because he was never afraid. He was never afraid because he never imagined the possibility of crashing.

Even at a young age, I believed crashing was inevitable. I never could ride a bike like Matt. Rushing down a dirt trail or driveway, flying off a jump, pushing myself over the line, I could never completely let go. I always imagined the crash. I always flinched, and I wonder if this is ultimately what defines the difference between Matt and me—that flinch of the imagination at work, that thinking-too-much I tend to do.

The Vasquez Creek, depending on the rains, is more of a river than a creek in some spots. One summer Dad, Matt, and I bought topographical maps of the region and scouted out a trail that would take us to the end of the valley and up to the Continental Divide. We rode part of the trail one day, just far enough to get a feel for the terrain and check out a couple of forks in the path. We rode back down that night, and a storm followed us in. It rained all night.

The next morning we packed up our gear, loaded the bikes on the trailer, and drove the truck up to a parking spot we had picked out. The sandy soil had already sucked up most of the water. We rode all day, taking time to play around in the creek and explore side trails. It was midafternoon when we made it to a creek crossing we'd scouted the day before.

The Vasquez Creek we expected to find was maybe a foot deep and meandering along the gravel beds. But that's not what was waiting for us after a night of rain. The water was now a good two or three feet deep and moving fast. Dad was on the 175, the biggest bike of the three. We all sat at the edge of the creek and talked about whether we should try the crossing or not. If we didn't, we'd have to turn around and go home. But if we did make it, we'd have to do it again on the way back down.

Eventually we decided to give it a shot. Dad backed up and raced his bike into the water, slipping a little, bogging down just slightly, but he made it through to the other side in fine shape. He parked his bike and walked down to the bank to help us.

I was next. I paused for a second and stared at the surging current, then backed up, shifted into first gear, and gunned my little 100 cc into the creek. Almost immediately I flinched, tensed up, and began to slip on the rocks. I was afraid. The current pushed over the seat, and my feet came off the pegs. The tailpipe went under and the engine started to bog down.

For a moment I was suspended there in the water, between Dad and Matt, between father and brother, struggling against the current, feeling it surge and push against my legs. The bike started to slip out from under me. I gunned the engine and dug my toes into the rocks, pushing with all I had, until I got close enough for Dad to grab the handlebars and pull me out of the water. He yanked and I pushed until we got the bike up on the bank. The engine sputtered dead.

Matt came next, without a pause, and raced into the water, standing up on the pegs and, light as he was, cruised through and out the other side without assistance. He didn't so much as pause. Where I had nearly been swept away by the current, Matt looked almost graceful, totally natural and unafraid.

• • •

During one of our family trips to Colorado, Dad finds this place called Strawberry Lake on a map after hearing stories from Uncle Rick. It's a long trip on a four-wheel-drive road, but Uncle Rick says it's worth the drive. So we pack up the little Toyota with one day's worth of provisions and set out for the lake, planning on a leisurely picnic and maybe a little trout fishing.

Mom and Dad are riding up front, while Matt and I buckle ourselves into the bus seat in the back. At first everything is great. We're just bouncing through the forest, following a road that seems to get worse and worse. The little truck is taking it just fine and we're enjoying the ride for a while. But the road just keeps going, and soon we've been bouncing for hours and still no Strawberry Lake. We dip down into a valley, trying to stay on a road that's now muddy and filled with giant holes.

I don't really start to worry until the truck slides off the road into a ditch. The front bumper presses up against a pine sapling. We're stuck. But we don't panic. Dad came prepared. He always does. He opens one of the ammo boxes bolted to the bed of the truck and pulls out a folding camp saw. Matt, Dad, and I each take a turn sawing and eventually cut the tree down to a stump, just low enough for us to get out.

There's no room to turn the truck around, so we just keep moving. The road parallels a wide field, where we start to see the occasional cow or two milling around with head down, tail swishing in the air. This seems like a good sign.

It's a ranch built up in the hills, and as we start to get closer to what seems to be the main house and outbuildings, we spot a large blue cylinder sitting next to the road. Stenciled on the side in big black letters are the words "Caution: Bear Trap." We roll past the thing, staring in awe. Remember, we're from Kansas. We don't really have predators—unless you count raptors, snakes, or the occasional coyote. Bears are a different story. Mom urges Dad to keep moving, while Matt and I wonder about giant, hungry bears lurking in the trees and leaping into the truck, gorging on fresh, pink, hairless boy-meat.

We just keep moving, and about a quarter of a mile down the road we are stopped at a large metal gate. We're not there long before a man and woman come rolling up in a truck. The man leans out of the passenger window and points a shotgun at us.

They both climb out of the truck, and the woman barks, "What the hell do you want?" Dad approaches cautiously at first, waving and smiling. He stops just in front of the truck and begins to explain to her how we've gotten lost trying to find Strawberry Lake.

"You're not hippies, are you?" she demands to know.

"No, ma'am. No hippies here," Dad says, pointing toward the truck. Matt and I stand up on cue and wave halfheartedly. Mom shows her face too.

"Goddamn hippies are always driving up to Strawberry Lake." The man just stands there with his gun raised at us. "They go skinny-dipping," she says.

"Ma'am, I can assure you we have no intention of doing anything like that," Dad says. He moves closer to her, taking slow, deliberate steps until he is out of my earshot. He and the woman talk for a little while longer, and then he comes trudging back to the pickup.

"She'll let us through," he says and starts the engine. "If it wasn't for you," he says, gesturing toward Matt and me, "she would have made us turn around. She felt sorry for you boys," he says, and we drive through the gate, past their house and barns, and down a winding road that leads out of the valley, back to the blacktop highway, and home. We never found Strawberry Lake, and we never tried again after that day.

• • •

One of our most familiar day trips out of Winter Park takes us over Corona Pass, an old railroad line connecting Denver and the Fraser Valley. We've come to know this road pretty well. We've explored the old ghost town of Arrow, which is just a few buried stone foundations and a graveyard hidden in the trees. We've been all over the hills in cars and on our motorcycles, and think of it as pretty safe terrain.

We know it well enough to know that, if you're on a bike, there are parts of the road you're better off avoiding. There's tourist traffic sometimes, and old railroad ties buried under the dirt will rattle the teeth out of your head. The switchbacks in the road are connected by trails. Matt and I stick mostly to these.

This one day we're on our motorcycles, coming down the pass into Winter Park. A light afternoon rain has begun to fall. Dad is driving his truck and will meet us back at the cabin. We see him once on the road and then lose sight of him. Matt crosses the road, and I follow him down another trail. Looking back over my shoulder, I realize we're moving away from the road that we need to follow. I start to panic.

Matt has a good lead on me and is riding hard. Dad always tells us to never lose each other. *Always stay together.* I shift gears and speed up, bouncing over rocks and roots, trying to catch him or at least get his attention. Matt is fast, and I follow him forever it seems. We stop the bikes, and I scream at him over the sputter of the engines. "We're going the wrong way. We'll be lost." He just waves me away, climbs back on his bike, and speeds off. I have no choice but to follow.

As much as I want to turn around and leave him out here in the woods, I can't do it. We're deep into a part of the mountain we've never scouted before. What would Dad say if I came back without my brother? Would he paint yellow signs and pound them into the ground? Would he remember this like the time I left Matt on the bus?

So I follow and curse Matt the whole time, convinced that by the time I get him to stop again, we will be so hopelessly lost we'll never get back to the road and will have to spend the night out in the woods. I do finally catch up to him as we're coming down a muddy hillside, but I slide out taking a turn and crumple my clutch pedal against an aspen tree.

By the time I get it bent back out with a rock, Matt is well ahead of me, sitting on his bike atop a nearby hill. As I pull up beside him, I am seething under my helmet, nearly spitting with rage. He just grins and points to the town of Fraser in the distance and below us the lodge for the small, privately owned ski area called Idlewild. He rides off down the ski run beneath a dormant blue chairlift. That son of a bitch, I think. He knows exactly where we are.

I follow him down the grassy slope, across the lawn in front of the ski lodge, into their gravel parking lot, and out the road that leads into the heart of Winter Park, only two blocks from the cabin and our father. We are miles from the Corona Pass road, and still I wonder if Matt knew all along, if he knew that all he had to do to get home was keep going, keep moving.

• • •

Matt never followed me, at least not in the normal ways. He always found his own path. While I was playing football and basketball, Matt took up BMX racing. He showed up at his first race wearing blue jeans, a T-shirt, and Dad's oversize motorcycle helmet. He lined up with the other kids and then blew them off the track.

Matt won without really trying. Soon he had a new bike and was racing in the competitive divisions, wearing the requisite brightly colored jersey, helmet, and pants. Matt spent many weekends at the tracks in Kansas City with Dad and quickly climbed the ranks until he was the top ranked rider in his age-group in Kansas and Missouri. He was nearly unbeatable.

He went to BMX Nationals in Oklahoma City one year, wrecked in the first turn, and still managed to finish in the middle of the pack. He brought home a trophy taller than he was. Sometimes I would go with Matt and Dad on the weekends, just to watch, and I loved to lose myself in that world, that culture of sport.

The parking lots were filled with families cooking out on hibachi grills and reclining in lounge chairs. Boys on bikes were everywhere. All different ages. All different sizes and abilities. Music trickled out of speakers. The boys rode wheelies around the parking lot and hopped around on their back wheels. They posed and preened and talked trash in front of the girls who fluttered around too—everyone buzzing on the same sort of vibe.

At home Matt was just my little brother—my pain in the ass little brother—but in this world he was a star. He beat everyone, and other kids hated him for it. He was characteristically fearless on the bike, but he was also a little mean and intimidating. Once in a tight race he was being crowded and jammed by another rider, and I watched him extend his foot mid-crank and kick the guy away from him, then rocket out in front of the pack and sky over a tabletop jump for the victory.

Matt asked my mom to stitch fabric letters onto the butt of his riding pants—something a lot of kids had done. Most of them just spelled out their names. Matt, however, emblazoned the phrase, "Bye Bye Sweetie Pie" on his butt so that the riders he passed would see his rear end and those words in their face. I tried so hard to talk him out of doing it, struggling to come up with all sorts of reasons why he couldn't put that on his pants, when the truth is I was envious of his arrogance, jealous of the confidence that would allow him to do such a thing.

This kind of confidence in my physical abilities wasn't something I found until much later on the basketball courts, and even then I never achieved the level of success that Matt did in BMX. I was never number 1, never the best in Kansas and Missouri, never even the best player on my team.

A couple of years after he started racing, Matt just quit. He got tired of it. So he took up road biking and would put in hundreds of miles a week on his bike. He entered mostly endurance races, completing an insane, sadistic race in Oklahoma, where he stayed on his bike for something like fifteen hours straight. He also rode the thrilling and glamorous Biking Across Kansas, which took him out on the long, flat highways of Kansas in the middle of the summer for ten days. It was like some twisted death march on bikes, but Matt loved every minute of it.

All of his extracurricular activities went like this. He just followed his own rhythm. For a while he took up skydiving and joined a team that performed in air shows. Instead of playing the trumpet or the trombone in school like I did, Matt played the baritone—this sort of half-tuba thing that meant he was typically one of two chairs in the band. But Matt actually practiced the thing—all the damn time it seemed—and played it well. Soon enough he won first at state band contests two years in a row. When they refused to let Matt play in the symphonic band unless he participated in marching band, he quit playing the baritone altogether. He told me he didn't want to wear one of those stupid uniforms, and that was it. He just quit and never looked back.

God, I wanted to be like that.

All I wanted was to be the best at something. I kept thinking that basketball was where I'd find my niche, my passion, and just the slightest taste of success on the court was as addictive as heroin. Matt, however, didn't really seem to care whether he was the best or not. He just *was* the best, and he didn't seem to need anyone else to recognize this. Sports and competition for Matt were something he did, not something he *needed*. I could never say the same.

• • •

As much as we had our own separate identities, Matt and I did a lot of things together that distinguished us from other kids. Our weekend outings with Dad were mini-vacations— full of fantastical new experiences like trips to junkyards and machine shops, shooting ranges, waterslides, and motorcycle parks.

One Saturday, Dad built us a spaceship.

Matt and I woke to find him in the garage surrounded by piles of two-by-four studs and sheets of plywood. The whole garage stunk of pine sap. Dad was absolutely glowing.

"Hey guys, what do you say we build us a Star Wars space-ship?" he said.

"An X-Wing Fighter?" I chirped.

"Of course," he said.

We spent most of the day in there. Dad drew out the plans on graph paper, showing us how to measure and mark straight lines, how to use T squares, levels, hammers, and saws. We cut and hammered, and hammered some more, and *Jesus* did we like hammering nails. Matt and I held contests to see who could sink a nail in the fewest strokes. Mine was always the brute-force approach, beating the nails into submission with my hammer, while Matt used efficient and graceful strokes to somehow sink nails artfully.

When we were finished, a fully built X-Wing Fighter replica lay on the floor of our garage, with a cockpit and navigator seat, wings made from two-by-six planks, and a pointed nose-cone section. It was a thing of beauty. Even Mom was impressed.

The next day we loaded it into the pickup and drove it down around the house into the backyard. Dad installed four posts to elevate the ship a few feet off the grass and built a ladder so we could climb into the cockpit from below. From then on, Matt and I spent hours flying in our own private spaceship, something I imagined other kids only dreamed about.

• • •

In many ways Matt is always more of a natural danger boy than I am. He trusts his instincts. For me, a lot of the fun of hanging with my dad and brother is just being outside, in the woods. There is this old pond we sneak off to—summer, winter, it doesn't matter the season—out on the edge of town, hidden down some old, rutted roads that twist past piles of junk people have dumped. There are refrigerators and mattresses, car batteries, and a water heater peppered with rusting buckshot wounds.

We back the Toyota up to the pond. Matt and I sit with our

rifles propped on the tailgate. Dad tosses an empty soda can out on the water and watches proudly as we compete to see who can sink it the fastest. The air rings with the sharp cracks of .22 rifle shots. Matt is a much better shot than I. He's calm, cool, and quick. He doesn't jerk the trigger, doesn't flinch. I've seen him pop poker chips from ridiculous distances.

In the winter the pond freezes solid. Dad skims beer bottles on the ice, we try to shoot them dead, and the air is punctuated again by rifle shots and a new seasonal sound—the sweet, hollow tinkling of an empty Miller bottle skipping across the frozen pond.

• • •

Our weekends weren't all guns and trucks and spaceships. Every Sunday, Matt and I dragged ourselves out of bed and Dad drove us to Plymouth Church for Sunday services. An assistant youth director for the church, Mom was usually there already, bright and early.

Some days we'd get Dad to stop for donuts on the way, but he almost always dropped us at the front door and drove away. Whenever I asked him why he didn't go to church with us, he said he had "done his time."

When we got home from church, we'd hang out with Dad, doing our danger boy activities while Mom worked around the house or ran errands. We'd often go shooting or riding or four-wheeling, but every now and then Dad would take us out for lunch at this big, sprawling bar called The Sanctuary.

At nights and on the weekends it was a college bar filled with drunken youths, but on Sunday afternoons it was often just a few regulars, Dad, Matt, and me. A few times it was just

Dad and me. They had video games, and Dad would feed me quarters while he bullshitted with the bartender and watched football.

The Sanctuary also had the best burgers in town, and I remember thinking how strange and wonderful it was to see the bartender disappear downstairs with our ticket in his hand and reappear ten minutes later with a burger and fries. This wasn't McDonald's. There was a grill somewhere in the building, and he was the only one using it. I'd sometimes eat two burgers, and the bar guys always marveled at my appetite.

The whole place stunk of beer and cigarettes. It was great. I loved hanging out there, watching sports and eating burgers with my dad, and there's part of me that looks for that kind of atmosphere in every bar. It's something like the feel of a British pub, a *family* drinking atmosphere.

• • •

Still, I can't deny that what I remember most about weekends with Dad was time spent on wheels and machines. The Toyota pickup became our group project. We cut out a hole in the cab and installed a sunroof one Saturday. Dad put in a tachometer and a custom-made roll bar welded at a local metal shop. The three of us dreamed of racing in the famous off-road races in the Baja desert. Dad even ordered racing harnesses that strapped crosswise over your chest and made it impossible to move.

We bought ammo boxes from the surplus store downtown and bolted them into the bed of the truck. We drove to a junkyard in search of a bench seat for the back. We carried our tools into an old, empty school bus buzzing with wasps, took

117

the seat, and barely made it out without getting stung. We bolted the seat in the bed of the truck, up against the cab, and installed belts so Matt and I could ride safely back there together with the boring adults up front.

• • •

Once when the three of us were riding in the Toyota, Dad spotted a dead fox on the side of the road and pulled over. Matt and I looked at him as if to say, "What the hell are you doing?" but he just climbed out of the truck. We followed as he sauntered over and toed the body with his boot, gently nudging the spine.

He bent down, poked the carcass with his finger, placed his hand in front of the fox's mouth to check for breathing, then stood up with a smile on his face. "It's fresh," he said. "Must have just been hit. Still warm."

Matt and I stared at him.

"It's beautiful," he said, and he was right. The fox was enormous, big as a German shepherd, and had a thick coat, deeply colored with rust orange, the ears tipped with white and black. "Let's keep it," he said.

"Huh?" I asked.

"Yeah, we'll take it somewhere and get it stuffed." Dad was grinning from ear to ear, and I couldn't tell if he was serious or not.

"What are you talking about?" I asked.

"We'll get it stuffed and take it home. We can put it in the living room." He stopped to admire the fox. "Oh shit, the dog will love it," he said, laughing at the thought.

"I don't know, Dad," I said. "We can't just take it."

"Sure we can," he said. "We'll throw it in the back of the truck. They'll just burn it up or throw it in the landfill anyway."

"Dad, please," I begged.

Matt smiled. "Let's do it," he said.

"No!" I barked. "We're not taking that thing."

"Okay, fine," Dad said, and we all climbed back in the truck. As we drove off in silence, I watched the fox recede in the mirror, and I was thankful we hadn't collected a carcass. But I also felt a little gutless and weak, as if I had missed a chance at adventure. I often felt this way around my dad and my brother.

• • •

When Dad's business is still going well, his company buys a field of corn on the south side of town with plans for a housing subdivision. He drives us out there in the Toyota one Sunday. It has rained recently, and the black soil sucks up to everything.

We drive off the road, up to the edge of the field. Matt and I are still not sure why we've come here, but we've grown used to this feeling of ignorance mixed with anticipation. We trust our father, even though it looks just like any other terraced field in Kansas—maybe a little smaller, since other subdivisions surround it.

Dad leans up on the steering wheel and grins at us. He punches the accelerator. The truck spins sideways, fishtailing out, and shoots forward, plowing through rows of corn—the stalks whacking up against the hood of the truck, which booms like a kettledrum.

We launch off a terrace and splash down in the mud and corn—all three of us screaming and yelling, getting bounced around inside the truck, slamming our heads on the ceiling. We mow down rows and rows, hitting the stalks just below the ears. They come flying up over the windshield and land in the bed of the truck.

When we are finished, much of the field lies broken and muddied. The truck is caked brown, and the bed is filled with ears of corn. We take it home, dry it out, grind it up in our electric flour mill, and Mom makes homemade corn bread.

• • •

When Matt and I joined the Boy Scouts, Dad became a troop leader. When we'd go on one of our camporees for a weekend, Dad would sometimes pull the pop-up trailer along and set it up nearby. One day I came back from some activity—knot tying, or map reading, or spear making—to find Dad and Matt camped out in lawn chairs in front of the pop-up, each of them puffing joyously on a fat cigar.

Dad's method of giving us whatever we asked for—beer, guns, and soft-core porn—had backfired with Matt. He actually liked smoking cigars. I tried it once, nearly lost a lung coughing, turned green, and vowed never to smoke again. Matt, however, enjoyed the flavor and physical actions of smoking. Dad would give him a puff every now and then when we were out shooting or four-wheeling. But this was the first time I'd seen Matt smoking his own cigar, and he seemed so proud of himself. He clearly liked seeing the smoke curl up from his lips into clouds around his head. Before long he could blow smoke rings too. I hated the smell and taste of cigar smoke, but there was part of me, seeing Matt and Dad puffing on stogies in lawn chairs, that longed to join them. It seemed like what I should do.

• • •

As I've said before, I was often the first one up around the house. So I was somewhat surprised early one winter morning when Dad woke me just after dawn. "Put on your snowsuit," he said with a gleam in his eye. "We're going sledding."

I peeked out the window to see only a couple of inches of snow. Oh well, I thought, it beats hanging out by myself. So I pulled my snowsuit out of the closet and climbed in. Bought through the JCPenney catalog, our suits were blue with yellow, and each one had a 1980 Lake Placid Winter Olympics patch Mom had stitched to the left arm.

"We have to go before it all melts," Dad says.

At this point I am scar-faced already from my bike wreck, black-toothed from a brick, still afraid of my fevers, and just last year Matt crashed his snow sled into a hedge thicket, punching a thorn right through his nose. At times, even *he* has started to seem fragile.

Still, we drag ourselves down to the garage, stopping to slip on Moon Boots in the mudroom. We all climb into the pickup. I look in the back. Dad has thrown the green Western Flyer saucer sled in the bed—a solid steel sled, the kind they now make out of pink plastic—and a coil of nylon ski rope.

The snow is not heavy, maybe only a couple of inches that will melt for sure when the sun comes up. Time is wasting, and the way Dad bounces with energy makes me consider the possibility that he has been up all night watching the snowfall,

121

waiting for this. We drive to a frozen terraced hayfield, land owned by the university and largely forgotten. We've come here before to go four-wheeling on the rutted-out dirt roads that wind around the property and up into a forested hillside just west of the aerospace buildings on campus.

When Dad stops the truck, all three of us climb out. Matt and I are still not completely sure why we have come to this field this morning. In addition to the lack of significant snowfall, it's not an especially nice spot to sled. There's no suitable hill to speak of, just a few gradual slopes and irrigation berms. But we trust our father. When he gets this look in his eye, we're rarely disappointed. So we just wait.

On the eastern horizon, over the roofs of the dormitories, the sun has just begun to pink the sky. The wooded hillside where they found a dead girl once is dappled in purple light. Dad beams and tosses the sled out onto the snow. It skims lightly across the surface, leaving a wide, flattened trail, before getting hung up on broken stalks of hay grass. He ties the ski rope to the bumper, lays it out on the ground, and ties the other end to the saucer sled. Matt and I shuffle around in the crisp snow, kicking dirt clods and snowballs. "Who's first?" Dad asks. It must be Matt who sits on the sled first, folds his legs under, and wraps his fingers over the front lip. Matt is always going first.

• • •

I'm the firstborn son, the older, bigger brother, who was supposed to do big things. But Matt, the second son, the little one, was the first son to leave home for college, the first to get out of Kansas. He was the first to shoot guns, ride a motorcycle, and jump out of an airplane; the first one to speak in tongues, first to win trophies too big for shelves, the first one between us boys to live a wild and fearless life. Matt was the first one to really live, and the first to wrap his car around a tree.

Matt was the first one to die.

He was eighteen years old.

After leaving the movie *Lethal Weapon 2* with a couple of friends, Matt lost control of his car in a turn, slid off the road, and slammed into a tree. He was killed almost instantly.

I always wonder if it was a final flinch, some tic of the imagination that pushed him over that line in the road. For once in his life, did Matt imagine the crash? Did he think too much? Or did he believe he could ride out the slide, will away the force of the impact? For some reason I always imagine that the road was sandy, and if I don't tune  it out, my memory is accompanied by the roar of rubber skating on the grains, tires barely touching the pavement, and then just this white-noise rush into black and a concussion like a grenade going off in my head. Was it fear or fearlessness that killed him? I'll never know. I can only imagine.

When my father's voice—of course it's *his* voice I hear, his voice I *need* to hear—comes to me over the telephone, I am asleep in Utah at a friend's house, one week into a West Coast road trip to see some Grateful Dead shows with Rachel. Half-conscious when he tells me, I don't believe him at first, hoping instead that this is some sick joke—sort of like the burnt leg destined for amputation or the fake knife in my gut. Maybe if I hold my breath long enough it will all disappear. But I know he wouldn't joke about something like this.

I fly home the next day for the funeral, spend a few days grieving with my family, and then fly back to Utah. I pick up my car, and just keep moving. Moving like Matt might move. Stubborn, fearless motion—driving, driving, and cutting through landscapes in my blue Subaru. Rachel and I. Slow and steady. We camp in sagebrush. We eat meals of canned ravioli cooked on a Coleman propane stove. We don't talk to people for days. We barely talk to each other. But I can't imagine being without her. We keep running, running, running with Kansas at our backs—trying to escape. And the desert lasts for years, the mountains hardly a distraction, and *Jesus* the ocean is so big and deep it won't let me forget.

• • •

Exactly one week after Matt's funeral, we are in a parking lot at a Grateful Dead concert and I have paid money to jump out of a 150-foot crane. The red basket jerks and raises slowly up off the asphalt, over the parking lot and crowds of Dead fans in homemade clothes and tie-dyed shirts. There are seas of unwashed, unkempt, and uninhibited people. The freaks are definitely out today. The beer crowd too. This is California, not Kansas anymore.

Nervous guys whisper out of the corners of their mouths,  "sheets, buds, shrooms," or "black hash, opium, sheets, sheets, sheets." It's always sheets of acid, and I can't help but see acid paper flapping in the breeze, strung out on a line behind an old house. Skinny, tanned white boys with dreadlocked hair roll a cooler on a skateboard chanting, "Sierra Nevada, Anchor Steam. Beer for a buck!" An innocent-looking girl who could be your sister or your neighbor wears a patchy homemade dress and hawks veggie burritos from a cardboard box.

I'm just seven days into the New World, and my ankles are bound in plastic boots and straps. I'm looking down at a sea of freaks. The basket swings from a cable—*rising, rising.* Just a few minutes ago, I watched a man in a fuzzy red bear costume do the same, waving to the crowd with his paws, smiling his costume smile.

The crane basket swings in the ocean breezes, swaying on a thin cable. Slowly we climb into the sky—the two jump "coaches" and me. I see down into the vast bowl of Shoreline Amphitheatre and watch roadies scurry around onstage, setting up amps and mics and drum kits. I see all the people in the parking lot, smaller now, waving at me like a field of Kansas wheat back home. And then it's the ocean lapping against the horizon, the sun stretched out hazy and yellow like a lemon drop. *Seventy-five. One hundred. One hundred fifty feet off the ground.* I've paid eighty dollars for 150 feet. These things cost money. They take sacrifice.

Swinging there in the middle of something huge, something I still can't quite see the edges of, I look at the black asphalt below, small patches of green grass here and there, the rolling seas of people, and a tiny red beanbag plopped down in the loading area—my landing pad.

One of the "coaches" checks the bungee cord hooked to my ankles while the other opens the small gate and points to a tiny metal step, barely big enough for my feet.

"Stand there," he says, and so I stand with my back to the basket.

I don't know why, but I'm not truly scared until he shuts the gate behind me and leaves me out there alone, perched at the edge, my fingers wrapped tight on the steel cage. And then the countdown begins. *Ten, nine, eight, seven.*

I'd like to tell you that I am thinking of my dead brother at this moment, that I am remembering the pictures I've seen of Matt wearing his skydiving flight suit, helmet, and safety goggles.

I'd like to tell you that I am grappling with deeper issues of mortality. I'd like to say that I'm feeling more than pure, unadulterated, adrenaline-charged fear. *Six, five, four.* And maybe I am. Maybe, subconsciously, I know there's no turning back now, no return to the life I lived before, the person I was before my brother died. But right now there is only one thing to do. *Three, two, one.*

Jump!

It takes forever to fall, and I love every terrifying second of it.

• • •

I wonder if, in those moments of ecstatic separation, that weightless free fall over the asphalt parking lot before the jerk back up into blue, I am living in the world where Matt lives now, where he has always lived.

• • •

After Matt was killed, they shipped his body home to Kansas, and the folks at McElwane's went to work fixing him up, patching his head, trying to make it look like he had just drifted off in his sleep and not crushed his skull against a tree.

I'd told my parents that I didn't want to see his body, that it was enough for me to know he was dead. I had tried to disengage from the details of his memorial service, finding it maddening to think about such mundane things. I thought I didn't want any say in the look of his gravestone but found myself sitting at home, stewing in my chair and twisting my fingers while my parents met with the funeral director. Time crawled around the clock. I tried to read, then watch television, but couldn't muster the concentration for either. Overcome with angst, I borrowed my grandparents' car and drove fast down to the funeral home. I parked the Cadillac in the lot outside and pushed my way through the large wooden doors.

I expected sweet-faced assistants or handlers with sympathetic voices to whisk me away. I expected someone to be there, to guide me where I needed to go. But there was nobody. Just an empty hallway with doors on either side. Not knowing where to find my parents, I stepped up to a set of glossy double doors and pulled on the handles, opening into a large room filled with chairs and red carpet runners.

At the front of the room was a shiny casket.

In the casket was my brother.

It took me a moment or two to understand that this was Matt and that I could no longer control whether I saw his body or not. I stood at the back of the room for some time, staring at the point of his nose peeking up over the rim of the casket, his pale forehead, and his dark brown hair. I almost turned around and ran, but something pulled me down the red carpet, right up to the edge.

Matt was laid out peacefully, hands crossed over his chest, and his face fixed up. They had put a lot of makeup on him, and he looked kind of pasty. He didn't look like he was sleeping. It's not that easy, this image. I reached out and touched the back of his hand. But it was so cold I recoiled as if I'd been burned. It felt like he had been dipped in liquid nitrogen. I suppose I had expected some lingering spark of life, some jolt of Matt's personality to come surging up my fingertips. Instead it was nothing. *Emptiness. Absence.*

I stumbled back, nearly falling off the raised platform where his casket sat, and ran out of the room. I pushed open several more doors, looking for my parents and finding nothing but more emptiness. I didn't tell anyone what had happened until much later.

My mom admitted that she had asked to see Matt's body, that she needed this for some measure of closure. She even picked out the clothes for him to wear. Somebody had to do it. Dad never did see him, and I wonder now if that's what keeps him more closely tied to Matt's grave site. Dad spends time there pruning the trees and planting flowers. I have trouble placing much importance on the grave, and part of the reason is because of that one quick touch. Somehow seeing his body, feeling the emptiness, allowed me to let go of the physical reality of his existence.

• • •

In the final accounting, what lives is what lingers in my mind, and this is it for me: we are together again, the three of us in a field of white snow, a saucer sled tied to the truck. It's cold. Dad and I lock in the wheel hubs and climb into the cab. Matt gives us the thumbs-up sign. Dad shifts into four-wheel drive and starts out slow. The sled bogs down a little in the snow, catching on patches of tall grass, but soon flies along behind the truck, skimming out over the frozen field like a puck on ice. I glance at the speedometer. It reads 15. Dad cranks the wheel and turns.

The sled swings out wide, g-forces ripping at Matt's snow-suit, and he actually lifts off the ground. I look in the mirror and see this blue boy flying for a split second on rope just barely tied to us, stretched out along the line between earth and sky, suspended there—before he comes down hard, bounces, and goes sailing head over heels through the snow.

He's a little slow to get up. It hurts to crash. Believe me, I know. But then he is all smiles, all action and buzz—that quick electric sensation of being separated from the earth, weight-less as if he's built with the hollow, airy bones of a bird. Matt jumps up, runs over to the sled, and climbs back on. He's forgotten all about the ground.

Dad smacks me on the knee and laughs, twisting his head back to see if Matt is ready behind us. He gives us the thumbs-up again. We drive fast over the terraces, whipping him out wide over the berms and snapping the sled back hard, letting him zip through the air and smack down again and again.

When Matt has finished, I will climb on the sled. I will do it because I want to, because it's expected of me, and because I trust my father. I will do it because I want to live like my brother lives, like Dad has taught us. I will do it because that's what danger boys do. There is no question, no blame, and no answer here. All that matters is the three of us burning tracks in the snow, tethered together, bound up in these moments.

Treading Water.

The duration record for treading water (vertical posture in an 8-foot square without touching the lane markers) is 64 hours by Norman Albert at Pennsylvania State University on November 1–4, 1978. (1980, 642)

Underwater.

The world record for voluntarily staying underwater is 13 minutes 42.5 seconds by Robert Foster, aged 32, an electronics technician of Richmond, California, who stayed under 10 feet of water in the swimming pool of the Bermuda Palms at San Rafael, California. (1980, 53)

Underground.

Reputedly the world's largest underground lake is the Lost Sea, which lies 300 feet underground in the Craighead Caverns, Sweetwater, Tennessee. Discovered in 1905, it covers an area of 4 1/2 acres. (1980, 147)

Well, Biggest.

After Matt dies it feels like I'm living underwater. I sort of disappear inside myself and occasionally come up for air. Some nights when I can't sleep or I'm just feeling anxious, I ride my bike to the cemetery where he's buried and jump the fence. I'm trying to find a connection, even if it's forced.

His grave marker is a flat granite bench. No headstone. It invites you to sit, rest your legs, and think—or not think—for a few minutes. It should be easier for me to be here. The cemetery is a quiet place full of history. Somewhere nearby is a mass grave for the victims of Quantrill's murderous raid. Up on the hill is the Catholic section, with its large, white statue of the Virgin Mary. Cicadas chatter at dusk, and you might hear the hum of a lawn mower in the distance if you come during the day. Squirrels scurry among the stones, gathering acorns. It's a solemn landscape, but every now and then, as I'm sitting there trying to be quiet and respectful, these silly lyrics play in my head:

> *The worms crawl in.*
> *The worms crawl out.*
> *The worms play pinochle on your snout.*

What does this mean? Am I an insensitive ass? I think I just don't know what to do besides laugh. My emotions are all fucked up anyway, and I find myself crying during AT&T commercials imploring me to "reach out and touch someone," bawling at dramatic moments in Olympic track and field events, and suffering panic attacks in my anthropology class, where it feels like I can't breathe.

• • •

I think about Matt all the time, but I rarely visit the cemetery. I always feel guilty for this later. After all, there was a cotton-wood tree planted near his grave because of something I wrote, a sort of eulogy steeped in Native American symbolism.

The minister used my words during the funeral. There was a lot of stuff about cottonwood trees and the circle of life. The problem is that cottonwoods grow best in sandy soil near rivers or lakes, and the dirt in the cemetery is thick, black clay. It's just not right.

Recently my father got a call from the cemetery caretaker telling him that the tree had to go. "It's not flourishing," he said. Of course it isn't, I think. It's a fucking cemetery. It's hard clay dirt. Nothing flourishes without proper roots.

• • •

I feel guilty for not taking the time to sit on Matt's headstone. But it's hard for me to feel much of a connection. I don't like thinking of my brother—and everything he is as a person—contained in the ground, limited to a wooden box, and sub-jected to the disregard of pinochle-playing worms.

Sure the bench is a nice monument and the graveyard is old and filled with giant oak trees, but it's still a contrived landscape of memory. It's just not the right place for remembrance. Matt and I never played in the cemetery, never rode our bikes down its winding, broken roads. That would have been strange.

Our memories were made in other places, other landscapes that seem more appropriate for a monument to his memory—like the mountains of Colorado or the lakes and streams of Kansas. I used to always say that when I died, I wanted to be propped up against a tree somewhere, maybe dressed in buckskin and clutching a rifle like that dead trapper in the movie *Jeremiah Johnson*. I'd also be holding a note that reads, "I kilt the bear that dun kilt me." I wanted a more natural death and a more abstract monument. When people visited my grave site, I wanted them to have to sign in for a backcountry permit, hire a team of mules, or paddle a canoe.

But perhaps there's more for me to learn in the cemetery. If I take the time to let my imagination work, perhaps there is a legacy of holes in my life, a pattern of strange monuments I have just begun to appreciate.

• • •

My paternal grandparents are buried in a cemetery that spreads out on the edge of Greensburg, Kansas. The town is named for a stagecoach driver, Cannonball Green. Granddad's and Grandma's graves are marked with flat stones, side by side, nothing too ostentatious but still dignified—just like their personalities.

The last time I was there was for my grandma's funeral. After they lowered her casket into the ground, I took a walk around the cemetery with Dad, and we stopped at another grave I'd seen once or twice before. It's a strange monument, a tiny, upright, coffin-shaped tombstone half buried in the dirt, no lid, with just a clear plastic window.

I kneeled down and pressed my face up to the window. Inside was a doll baby, a child's toy, planted in the dirt. She showed signs of age and neglect. Mildew crept over her plastic toes, fingers of moss snaked up her chubby legs—so that in some places there was hardly a distinction between dirt and doll. The window was beaded with condensation. One eyelid flopped down, only a few scattered lashes left. The other was pried open. She seemed to be thrust up through the soil, suspended there for me to see.

"Man, that's creepy," I said as I stood up.

"Yeah," Dad said, but he was already walking away, back toward the car.

I'd seen this monument before—but it still kind of freaked me out. Obviously the grave of a dead child, it made me wonder about the kind of grief a parent must suffer when he loses a child. Maybe it's the sort of pain that needs crass and confrontational raw-nerve monuments—headstones with doll babies, loudspeakers, cuckoo clocks, and screeching alarm systems.

• • •

Greensburg is a town full of strange monuments to both life and death. Another headstone in the same cemetery holds a hardtack biscuit from the Civil War—obviously outliving the man who stashed it for years. Two blocks from the cemetery, their city pool sports an Olympic-size diving tower at one end, numerous boards and slides, and even an island in the middle. It's a big, watery oasis sloshing in the middle of a flat, dusty plain, and during the hottest days of summer, the whole town seemed to swim in its sustenance. A giant, blue-bottomed monument to water, the lifeblood of the high plains, a facility built to foster Olympic dreams perhaps, it certainly dwarfed any pool I had ever seen.

During our yearly trips to visit the grandparents, Matt and I often sought summer shelter at the Greensburg pool. We believed we had found some watery heaven there, a welcome escape from the boredom and heat of Western Kansas. We leaped from concrete towers and tucked into cannonball form. We swam beneath the island, imagining ourselves in some undersea adventure. It seemed like a grave injustice to us that Greensburg, of all places, would have a bigger, better pool than our hometown.

• • •

Though I claim to feel little connection to Matt's grave site, I remember the anger that welled up inside me when the caretaker called me at work one day to tell me that vandals had struck the cemetery.

They had toppled stones and obelisks, striking a path of destruction that inevitably crossed Matt's monument. They had picked up a granite vase and cracked it over his bench, probably hoping to break it, but only took a chip out of the flat top, scarring up the circle surrounding the inscription.

My parents quickly offered a reward for information leading to the arrest of the vandals, and I imagined hiding out in the cemetery at night, waiting for them to return and exacting some kind of violent revenge with hammers or a baseball bat. I'd have an open grave nearby, just waiting, and I'd dump them in, throw a couple of shovels of dirt on them, and leave.

I'd rather have worms playing cards on Matt's snout than teenage vandals terrorizing the surface of his grave. You don't have to appreciate monuments, but you have to respect them. They are objects that have gathered meaning and put on the weight of memory. We build gravestones out of granite not just because it is the most weather-resistant stone but because it is the heaviest and strongest. It weighs almost as much as a life. It weighs about as much as the grief you carry around after someone dies—like a whole swimming pool full of water above you.

Days and weeks pass without a word from the authorities. I call the caretaker a few times just to inquire. My parents increase the award amount. It's a few hundred dollars, enough you'd think to make some kid come forward, but all the families of the deceased are forced to pay for repairs to their headstones. Eventually you get used to living underwater, but you never shed the weight completely.

• • •

From the Greensburg cemetery or the pool, from anywhere in town really, you can see the biggest monument around, a green-and-white water tower marked with black letters BIG WELL. It's the tallest structure in town—besides maybe the grain silo—and its primary function seems to be as a billboard for the real attraction, a giant hole in the ground. Hand-painted signs outside town advertise the "World's Largest Hand-Dug Well," but I can find no mention of it in the Guinness Books. Believe me, I've looked.

World Record or not, the Big Well is truly an impressive hole. Thirty-six feet in diameter, 109 feet deep, it was originally dug to supply water for the railroad. The Ogallala Aquifer sits beneath the Western Kansas plains—a massive underground freshwater sea spreading from Nebraska to Texas—and the Big Well punches straight down into the aquifer.

After the railroad started using diesel engines, the well provided drinking water for the town. But now the Big Well just draws the occasional tourist or trucker flying through town on Highway 54. I spent a lot of time hanging out at the gift shop. The old ladies who worked there were nice and didn't seem to mind me loitering around the premises.

Tractor trailers and RV's sometimes stopped. People piled out and flowed around the gift shop. They peered down through the windows over the Big Well, their faces pressed up against the dirty glass, but they rarely went further. The tourists stuck to the safe confines of the gift shop, where they bought souvenir combs, shot glasses, oversize pencils, and blocks of cedar painted with rhyming poems and shellacked to a high gloss. They bought ceramic bells, painted saw blades, thimbles, spoons, and coffee mugs with their names on them: Earl, Bertha, Willie, and Sam. They bought lots of things to prove they had stopped. They bought tiny portable monuments to carry home.

I watched the tourists, and most of them never made the trip underground, down into the Big Well, past the surface monument. Perhaps it was the stacked-stone walls that worried them, or the shaky look of the blue metal staircase. Maybe it was a reluctance to move past a surface-level recognition. I can understand this. But I've stood at the bottom and gazed up at the walls, stones cut by hand, carried by hand, and stacked by hand. No backhoes or bulldozers. Just muscle and shovels. And I never worried. Not once. I felt at home.

Standing in the Big Well is like standing at the bottom of a massive drinking straw, this hand-carved hole in the high plains, a portal to another world. There at the bottom, I felt close to the organs of the earth. I saw water from the aquifer now sealed off in the Big Well—green and mossy, with goldfish swimming just beneath the skin. I saw their bony backs wiggling through my veins, pushing their way into my organs.

I imagined the ugly surface above me, crop fields and clogged highways, cities and forests of sturdy killer trees, everything resembling a thick, protective coating of scar tissue. Cars buzzing around in their painted shells, sliding on the sand. I peeled it all back and found an ocean beneath the surface, waves lapping up against fresh, pink mountains and shores of new geologic flesh.

• • •

I still wonder what there is to learn at the bottom of the Big Well about living. Down past the moss and goldfish, there's a window out onto another world beneath the skin, a better world. I can just imagine vast cavities of space under the surface, room to build cities, room to sit on shores, skipping pebbles on an underground sea. The air down there is cool, a constant forty degrees year-round. It takes some time for my eyes to adjust to the dark. They go pink and bulge from my skull. But in the dim light, I look up to see what seem, at first, to be stalactites but what materialize into thousands of water wells and irrigation sprinklers, all punched down through the skin like mosquito needles plumbed straight to a vein.

Every community, every family feeds off the aquifer. Without it there is no wheat, no soy, no milo or corn; there is no food for tables, no clothes for backs. There is no life. There is no Olympic-size swimming pool. Without the water—a finite resource—the towns of Southwest Kansas would probably just dry up and blow away. Thus *life* here is a finite resource. Always. If you live on the surface, in the real world, you try not to think about this. You try not to think about that raspy, sucking sound of a straw hitting the empty bottom of a cup, or the scrape of a gravedigger's shovel.

From where I sit on the underground shores, I can see the underside of the surface world I've just barely known, hardly appreciated. I can see the legacy of holes in my family, the pattern of loss, and the monuments we build to them.

Somewhere on this aquifer my grandfather is still fishing with his friend Punk Justus. They catch stringers of extinct species. Somewhere down there my brother water skis with dead Kennedys. His casket in Eastern Kansas is just another door. He skydives from Amelia Earhart's airplane. He sits in a lawn chair smoking a cigar with the great-uncle I never knew, the one who died in his car.

Everyone is here, even my cousins who died as kids. They paddle on an air mattress in the dim light. Benny and Billy Mc-Crary lounge in some Adirondack chairs, talking with my maternal grandma. She's drinking vodka and orange juice. My other grandmother runs the family Cadillac like a bandit, catching air over rises on the dusty side roads. She asks me if I want a lift and jerks her thumb at the backseat. Over by the water, my maternal grandpa Doc sells lamps from his station wagon. He stops and sits for Osceola cheese and green apples on a wooden deck.

All the dead heroes have weekend houses here. All the dead heroes float pontoon boats in the annual Fourth of July parade. All the dead heroes are waiting for me. I kick my shoes off on the rocks, wade out until my toes won't touch, and I'm treading water on the underground sea, just barely afloat.

Showering.

The most prolonged continuous shower bath on record is one of 336 hours by Arron Marshall of Rockingham Park, Western Australia, July 29–August 12, 1978.

Desquamation*can be a positive danger. (1980, 480)

Skin, Toughest.

Arron Marshall could have cleaned himself to death. I didn't want to go that far, but there were days I wanted to wash myself down the pipes. It takes time to do this, but first the skin would prune and pucker, then start to break down and peel off in thin sheets. It would turn gray and slimy, and might get hung up in the drain trap before I disappeared completely.

It's not easy to make this sort of change.

I wonder about Arron's urge to molt, to shed skin and self, and I imagine his emergence from the shower, all pink and raw like a skinned animal—nerve endings, veins, and blood vessels barely hidden beneath his last few remaining surface layers— he'd look like one of those anatomical science dolls just waiting to be dissected. The wind would hurt when it blew. That's the way grief works. Simple noises, black cars, trees, a few words—the flotsam of daily life—sink you down again. When your skin is as thin as Arron's, it takes only one touch from a fingernail to split you wide open.

It's maybe a few months after we put Matt in the ground, and I've gone to the bank to make a deposit. I'm standing in line when I see the mother of a childhood friend approaching from across the lobby. She wears a long denim dress and this weird little pixie haircut. Her head tilts to the side when she sees me—an involuntary movement of sympathy I've seen many others make. She hugs me tight and holds my hands in hers, looking up at me with her lips pursed. People around us start to stare.

"Oh, Steve. I'm so sorry about Matt," she says. "How are you?"

"You know," I say, "hanging in there." I look around the lobby, feeling rather self-conscious. I start to sweat a little. I never know what to say.

"Well, you know God must have had a better use for Matt in Heaven," she says, her words cutting into me. "He must have needed him more than we do."

I just sort of stare at her. I don't know what to say. It's all I can do not to explode. I mean literally explode—splattering my guts and bones and brains all over that bank lobby. I'm close to that. But I just sort of nod and smile. I don't tell her about my swimming excursions on the underground sea, or how much *I* need my brother.

"Uh, yeah," I say, "I suppose so," wishing that she had just kept her mouth shut. That's what most people do. They don't know what to say, so they don't say anything. When this is over, I want to mail her a postcard that simply reads, "Silence can be a good thing."

She stares at me for a few more seconds, then shakes my hands with her sweaty Jesus palms and tells me to take care of myself. Then she's gone and I'm still standing in line at the goddamn bank, trying not to burst into tears.

• • •

Arron Marshall must have been a little nuts. I mean, who showers for fourteen days without having a few screws loose? But you have to admire him too—just a little bit. You have to admire his ability to take what was given to him—his compulsions, his pain, his possible grief—and turn it into something else, some positive, something World Record worthy. That's big. That's powerful. In my book, he's taken self-improvement to a whole new level. After Matt dies, I can feel the grief pulling at me, dragging me under, and I want to wash away layers of self too and grow new leathery-tough skin, the kind of protective covering I need to survive.

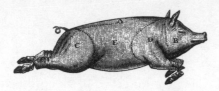

The world's greatest trencherman is Edward Abraham
("Bozo") Miller (born 1909) of Oakland, California. He con-
sumes up to 25,000 calories per day, or more than 11 times
that recommended. He stands 5 feet 7 inches tall but weighs
from 280 to 300 lbs., with a 57-inch waist. He has been
undefeated in eating contests since 1931. (1980, 489)

Chicken.

27 (2-lb. pullets) by "Bozo" Miller . . .
at a sitting at Trader Vic's, San Francisco,
California, in 1963. (1980, 489)

Ravioli.

324 (first 250 in 70 minutes) by "Bozo" Miller . . . at Rendez-
vous Room, Oakland, California, in 1963. (1980, 491)

Swallowing.

The worst reported case of compulsive swallowing was an
insane woman, Mrs. H., aged 42, who complained of a "slight
abdominal pain." She was found to have 2,533 objects in her
stomach, including 947 bent pins. (1980, 44)

Trenchermen, World's Greatest.

I love to eat—always have—and I understand that some people like Mrs. H. eat to fill up emptiness in the heart or mind, some deep well inside. I understand that eating can be a physical addiction, and perhaps that's true for me as well. Though I'm not obese, I do have the potential to be that way—a combination of excessive eating habits and body type—but so far I've been able to maintain a balance.

As much as I love to eat, my body doesn't always appreciate it. My stomach is weak and prone to illness. I was a colicky baby, and sometimes I'm a colicky adult. I can't hold my liquor. My gut just doesn't share my appreciation for bratwurst or a bowl of cereal at 10:00 P.M. There's a disconnect, a miscommunication with my brain, and my stomach often awakens me at 3:00 A.M. just to punish me for that bag of chips, those ten cookies, and that half pint of Ben & Jerry's coconut almond fudge chip ice cream. It's a vicious, masochistic cycle.

I know there are times I eat for comfort, and I also know that the root meaning of the word *worry* is "to devour, to consume." This means, of course, that worry will devour you— sort of like a parasite eating away from the inside, or maybe like me gnawing away at my own fingernails until they're bitten down to nothing, and then chewing on the fleshy tips of my fingers, consuming tiny bits of myself, just for something to do instead of worrying.

But for me this also means that "to worry" is an attempt to control the world around me, an effort to devour harm, insecurity, and pain. So perhaps eating for me is an outward, physical manifestation of an inward worrying. It's a search for self, the visible expression of my attempts to understand how I fit in the world.

This must have been true for Mrs. H. too—but on a different level. I can't help but imagine her sitting at her small, round kitchen table, a glass of milk in front of her and a pile of straight pins—the kind with the little colored balls on the ends. She wears a bathrobe. It's the middle of the night. A forty-watt bulb casts a yellowish glow over her. The soundtrack from *The Big Chill* plays on the hi-fi. She methodically picks up a pin, bends it in half, places it on the back of her tongue, takes a gulp of milk, and swallows it down.

She does this 947 times.

• • •

People often ask the same question when I confess my obsession with *The Guinness Book of World Records*. "Have you set a record?" they will ask, and then I feel the need to clarify—not just for them but for me too. It's not that I'm obsessed with setting records. There's a man named Ashrita Furman who holds the Guinness Record (eighty-two) for holding the most Guinness Records. *He's* obsessed with setting and breaking records.

Among his many other achievements, Mr. Furman happens to be the current holder of several pogo-sticking titles, and the truth is I find myself resenting his competitive drive. He has a spiritual mentor named Sri Chinmoy, who appears to be some sort of weight lifter. He has a fancy website featuring pictures of Mr. Chinmoy and Mr. Furman, a blurb from Regis Philbin, and another from *The Christian Science Monitor* that mentions Ashrita in the same breath as Muhammad Ali, Michael Jordan, and Babe Ruth. But that just seems to take it a bit too far, doesn't it? Quite honestly, I have some trouble with the fact that his path to enlightenment is all about breaking records, setting new records, and generally hogging all the fame.

Just like I wanted to knock my little brother off his pogo stick, I'd have the urge to do the same to Mr. Furman if he came bouncing past me on the street. There could be some kid out there like Michael Barban or Scott Spencer who really likes his pogo stick and thinks maybe he could set some kind of record. But when he looks in the Guinness Book, he sees Ashrita Furman's name plastered all over the pogo stick section. He'd probably just give up his dreams for a World Record and start shoplifting or slinging crack or making crystal meth in a storage garage. . . . It could happen.

Okay, so my obsession is not with breaking records but with record holders, with *people*. More specifically, I'm obsessed with the people in *my* editions, 1980 and 1982, of the Guinness Book. They sort of moved into my psychic space when I was a kid and never left.

That's not to say I haven't thought about trying to set a record. But there's something about the whole process that puts me off. I'm just not sure I'd have the commitment or the discipline. I'm not sure I'm willing to make that kind of sacrifice.

In junior high school I did set a school record for consuming cafeteria cinnamon rolls by eating eight of them during one lunch period. But it didn't take much commitment or sacrifice, and I wasn't really trying to set a record. I just liked eating cinnamon rolls, and I figured if these kids were stupid enough to trade me their cinnamon rolls for dishes of canned corn, then I might as well take them. As much as I've always enjoyed eating, I've never had the urge to compete at it, at least not in any organized way.

• • •

My dad and I both have big barrel torsos and wide shoulders. We're each strong, even somewhat imposing, but not obviously athletic or muscled. *Thick* is a word that seems to describe us pretty well. It's the standard body characteristic in Dad's family, and this often made our holiday gatherings look like reunions of the 1969 Kansas City Chiefs.

Dad likes to say about his pants, "I wear a thirty-eight-inch waist. But a forty felt so good, I bought a forty-two."

When I was growing up, he never played golf or softball with friends, the kinds of things other dads did to socialize and exercise. He never drank or smoked or did much of anything else to excess—unless it was working or eating. He used to amaze us at the dinner table with Guinness-like feats of eating. He'd stab a canned pear half dripping in syrup and slide the whole thing into his mouth while Matt and I stared at the fruit on our own plates and wondered if we'd ever live up to this heroic act. He'd tell stories about when he was a kid and he'd happily eat cow brains for breakfast and tongue for dinner—as if it was nothing at all. He could inhale a bucket of fried chicken gizzards in a matter of minutes. An open bag of chips was an empty bag of chips.

When my mother made gravy with dinner, dessert with Dad meant crumbling bread on a plate and soaking it in the leftover gravy. He'd make a pile bigger than my head, and it was usually just the two of us sitting there, forking soggy lumps of bread into our mouths. Mom and Matt had little interest in leftover gravy. But I remember the warmth in that connection Dad and I had over gravy bread, that strange, silent intimacy among men. We also shared late nights watching the occasional episode of *Hawaii Five-O* or *The Six Million Dollar Man.*

Eats Fast and Eats Everything: **Peter Dowdeswell of England holds the records in 10 categories: beer, eels, eggs (hard, soft and raw), pancakes, potatoes, prunes, sandwiches (shown here) and shrimps. He plans to try for lemons and gherkins soon. (1982, 502)**

In the black-and-white photograph from my 1980 Super-Edition, Peter Dowdeswell crams a sandwich into his mouth with a thick, tattooed left arm. He wears a black cowboy hat. Behind him hangs a hand-painted sign that reads "The Donut Shop Sandwich (Eating) Record Attempt." Next to him on a chair sits a small, blond child, maybe a boy, with his legs barely long enough to hang off the chair. He sits next to his dad, leans over the table toward his destiny, and shoves a piece of sandwich into his mouth.

I don't want to blame my father for my overindulgent eating habits or for my size. I want to thank him. Like it or not, they're part of who I am. Still, today I can't go to a buffet without eating until I feel ill. I like to pretend that it's some sort of social contract I agree to when I set foot in a buffet, this unwritten duty to eat until I bust—but I suspect the truth is less noble.

I suspect my father and I could have been like Peter Dowdeswell and his boy. We could've been World Record holding trenchermen, a father-son eating machine. When my friends and I get together today, we eat and we remember eating. We tell stories about amazing enchiladas at shady Mexican restaurants, stolen barbecue grills, homemade sausage, and smarmy waitresses who doubted our ability to finish the Big Breakfast, the Miner's Plate, the Minturn Loop—whatever they happen to be calling the biggest combo meal on the menu. My dad used to say that I ate "like someone was going to take it away from me." And I do sometimes. There's a strange surge of competitive juices that still causes me to envy other men at the buffet—their plates piled high with crab shells and bones, noodles and fried wontons.

I suspect I would have led the cannibalistic charge with Packer and Donner and that soccer team in the Andes. I would have been a mean old carcass-thieving caveman. But I am a little older now—thirty-two this year—and my metabolism is slowing down to keep pace with the deterioration of my knees. Every now and then I have a fleeting image of my future, this hazy time when I must concern myself with not just the *quantity* but also the *quality* of food I eat. I'm a father now and must set an example for my child—one that doesn't lead him down the deep-fried path, the gravy road, or the seductive sausage highway.

Lightest Humans. **The lightest recorded adult was Lucia
Zarate, born in San Carlos, Mexico, on January 2, 1863.
At birth she weighed 2.5 lbs. This emaciated ateliotic dwarf
of 26 1/2 inches weighed 4.7 lbs. at the age of 17. She
"fattened up" to 13 lbs. by her 20th birthday. She died in
October, 1889.**

**It was recorded that the American exhibitionist Rosa Lee
Plemons (born 1873) weighed 27 lbs. at the age of 18.
(1980, 20)**

My wife is barely five feet tall, though I swear I never really notice she's that much smaller than I am. One of the only times
our size difference becomes obvious is when I eat meals with
Rachel and her parents. They are kind and wonderful people,
but they are small people with small appetites who live in a decidedly anti-Guinness world.

It's summertime in Kansas, the middle of August, and I'm
eating dinner with Rachel's parents for one of the first times. I
feel like I'm sort of trying out for her mom—even though
there's really no turning back for Rachel and me now—and I
want to make a good impression.

The whole house is filled with colorful Turkish rugs and
smells of garlic. I have to leave my shoes at the door. Rachel's
stepdad offers me slippers, but they don't have any that fit me,
so I just go barefoot. Her mother has made some kind of
chicken dish that's cooked in a clay pot with forty cloves of garlic, and it smells absolutely amazing.

I'm hungrier than I thought I was, and my belly burbles as I
sit down next to Rachel at the table. Her mom hands me a

bowl of red lentils, and I set it down next to my plate, thinking it's for me alone. Just as I'm about to dip my spoon in and take a bite, Rachel elbows me in the ribs.

"Pass the bowl," she whispers.

"Huh?"

"The lentils," she says. "Pass them. They're for everyone."

I immediately grab the bowl and hand it to Rachel, mouthing the word *thanks* as her parents sit down opposite us. As delicious as the chicken looks and smells, I make a conscious effort not to fill my plate with food. I don't shovel but calmly cut bites of chicken and place them in my mouth.

I try to make a good impression, but it's hard.

Rachel's stepfather (bless his patient soul) eats like a bird, a very tiny bird, and I find myself hovering over his plate after I've finished my modest portions, watching him cut small bites and slowly fork them into his mouth. He could set records for Longest Mastication, Persistent Chewing, or Patient Digestion.

I try to step outside of myself, forget my need to feed, and see it as a learning experience, a test of my patience and my ability to mold my own desires to someone else's world. But it's a world where trenchermen are not welcome, where indulgence is measured on a different scale. My stomach rumbles, and I feel huge and culturally ignorant—like an anthropologist communing with the natives. We live in different skins. We travel in different orbits.

On the weekends Rachel's parents paddle a miniature canoe; they both wear tiny, hand-woven slippers imported from a Mediterranean country. Bus travel for them is a breeze.

Their kitchen cabinets contain boxes with three crackers, a dozen peanuts, and a handful of chips—anomalies I've never actually witnessed in my own cabinets.

It's true that at times I feel strangely like the shipwrecked Gulliver around them, and I worry that some morning I may wake to find myself tied to the bedroom floor with piano wire—the little people dancing around my bed, singing songs of victory.

Most Accurate Shooting (basketball).

In a 24-hour period, May 31–June 1, 1975, Fred L. Newman of San Jose, California, scored 12,874 baskets out of 13,116 attempts (98.15 percent). Newman has also made 88 consecutive free throws while blindfolded at the Central Y.M.C.A., San Jose, California, February 5, 1978. (1980, 524)

Joints, Weakest.

It's hot outside and sticky-humid, so I've come to the air-conditioned rec center to escape and play some pickup basketball. I get in a good game of five-on-five right off the bat, and I'm running well, keeping up on the break, making some jump shots from the outside. I start to get a bit tired during the third game, but I catch my second wind and feel like I can go for a while longer. I'm posting up strong, drop-stepping to the basket, and hitting hook shots. I still have my legs under me when I jump, and my back feels good.

It's just great to be on the court again. I'm finally starting to feel healthy and whole again—maybe for the first time since Matt died. I'm starting to feel rebuilt. *Bigger. Stronger. Faster.* At times even fearless and invincible. Sometimes when I'm playing, I get this kind of rush that must be similar to the mythical "runner's high," and I feel lighter, positively *bionic*, as if I'm skating over the surface of the court on a cushion of air, moving with electronically enhanced, unrealistic grace. I can almost hear the bionic beeping of my retooled circuits.

The game is close, just a few points separating the teams, so guys are playing hard, banging around in the lane. Someone chucks up a long three-pointer, and it bounces off the front of the rim, flies over my head, drops, and rolls across the floor. I run toward the ball, plant my right foot, and lunge to grab it. My whole knee buckles and shifts forward, and I crumple to the hardwood.

At first I think it's just a knee sprain. It hurts bad, but I never hear the telltale popping sound that so many others report when they tear their anterior cruciate ligament. I even walk back to my car, and it's not until later that night, when I return to my little cabin-home, that my knee swells to the size of a cantaloupe and begins to pulse and throb with pain I've never experienced or even imagined. I eat aspirin like candy and still can't sleep. By the time I make it to the doctor the next day, I can't put any pressure at all on my right leg. It hurts so bad I can't think straight. I can barely focus on anything but my body.

Just when I was starting to regain that sense of invincibility, starting to feel comfortable in my own skin, my body rebels again and I begin coming apart at the seams—my stitches popping loose, my bolts rusting out, my ligaments shredding. My body rises up in revolt and reminds me again of its independent and violent will.

After the reconstructive surgery, I feel pain that I can't possibly describe, pain without metaphor that leaves me squeezing the couch and screaming into the cushions. At my most melodramatic moments during recovery, I want to *die* it hurts so bad. Literally die. I can't read, can't write. I don't sleep well. I can barely walk, even with my crutches. The pills they gave me hardly take the edge off and leave me stupefied and sleepy. But the worst part is I can't even *enjoy* feeling stupefied and sleepy because I need them too much for the pain. I even have to call the doctor and beg him for more. It's the kind of pain that makes me want to curl inside myself.

Believe it or not, the hardest part wasn't the physical healing. That just took some time and effort. It was the psychological mending that taxed me the most. Basketball had been great therapy for me, and my injury took that away. I got fatter than I'd ever been, putting on at least forty pounds during recovery, and I kind of disappeared into deep oceans of Hume and Kant and Mill as I tried to navigate my philosophy classes.

It took me a year or more just to step foot on a court again, months after that before I felt comfortable enough to play with other people. My knee still doesn't work quite right and makes funny popping noises. I can't walk down stairs the same as I used to. I have to take them slow. I buy soft-soled shoes that are just one step away from orthopedic footwear. Now when I hold my son on my hip, or carry him on my back, and feel that sting of pain in my knee, I find myself hoping that the future will bring cheap bionic joints and I can be rebuilt once again.

• • •

Many of my father's lessons in basketball involved teaching me how to take advantage of my strengths and minimize the effect of my weaknesses. After I made the eighth-grade team, Dad seemed to know that I would never be the quickest kid on the court and that I would never wow the crowd with my leaping and shot-blocking abilities. He understood that I would have to learn how to use my body to my advantage. But I can't help but wonder now if Dad also knew that I might find my own escape, my own refuge in the world of sports—something to get me out of my own head for a while, something to make me feel strong and successful. He probably knew I needed that, especially after I had to watch Matt skyrocket to the top of his class in BMX racing.

We're standing in the driveway. Matt's probably downstairs doing his homework or practicing his baritone. "The butt," Dad says, slapping his ass and dribbling the ball, "is the big man's best friend," and he backs into me with his rear end lowered and his legs spread, shoving me under the basket in our driveway. I shove back, wedging my knee into his legs and messing with his balance—just like he taught me. But he just shoves his butt into me harder, knocking me backward, until he has an easy layup.

"You have to take up space, son. You have to own the paint," he says, referring to the painted lane area on the court. "If any little guard or some other prick comes into your house," he says pointing at the area, "you better let them know about it. This is your *house!*"

Dad disappears into the garage while I shoot baskets, working on my footwork and follow-through. He reappears with this ring-like contraption and ladder. He climbs up the ladder and affixes the contraption over the rim.

"What the hell is that?" I ask.

"It's a *rebounder*," he says as he climbs down the ladder. "It won't let the ball go in the hoop. It's so you can practice your rebounding."

I stand there dribbling the ball. "That's a lot of fun," I say.

"Yeah, well, it's not all about fun," Dad says as he swats the ball out of my hands and fires up a jump shot that clangs off the rebounder. "You can't expect that they're going to treat you special out there. They're not just going to give you the ball."

161

He pauses to plant his foot, pivot, and launch a turnaround shot that bounces off the rebounder. "You have to take it," he says as he steps in front of me and shoves his butt into my hip, knocking me sideways, and grabs the ball out of the air.

"No matter what happens," he says, "you can always rebound."

Origins. ***Ollamalitzli*** **was a 16th-century Aztec precursor to basketball played in Mexico. If the solid rubber ball was put through a fixed stone ring placed high on one side of the stadium, the player was entitled to the clothing of all the spectators. The captain of the losing team often lost his head (by execution). Another game played much earlier, in the 10th century B.C. by the Olmecs in Mexico, called *Pok-ta-Pok*, also resembled basketball in its concept of a ring through which a round object was passed. (1980, 523)**

I was part of numerous losing efforts in basketball, but fortunately I never witnessed any beheadings. I was also never showered with panties and bras, skirts, stockings, and boots. I do like the idea of each game being imbued with such cultural, even spiritual significance. I like that each goal scored is, quite literally, a matter of life and death. Think how popular you'd be in the halls at school if you'd scored the basket that resulted in a sacrificial shower of clothing and a ritualistic decapitation.

Basketball didn't make me popular or less socially awkward in high school, but it was an escape from those pressures. Basketball was always an escape, an obsession of sorts. Our driveway was a fantasy world where I imagined myself hitting game-winning shots and being carried off the court by adoring and accepting teammates. Girls would swoon and perhaps consider chucking their underpants in my direction. But that was fantasy.

By the time I reached my junior year of high school, I was, in *reality,* one of the shortest and slowest starting post players in the state, but I compensated by also being one of the meanest and most competitive. They listed me at 6'5", and that's a pretty serious exaggeration, but I sort of reveled in the fact that I wasn't always the biggest kid, relishing my role as the underdog. A lot of people underestimated me on the court, and that was usually a mistake. After a game once in high school we found a handwritten sheet of scouting reports an opposing coach had left under the bleachers. Next to my name it said, "Slow but very physical. Can hurt you if you let him."

But even with all the pushing and shoving, you can't play basketball without a certain amount of grace and rhythm. Most people don't see the beauty of the game, the art of the movement. It's a dance.

> Drop step, lead with your elbows.
> Now plant, and rise, and extend.
> Drop step. Spin.
> Pump fake. Rise.
> Extend and flip.

It's all about footwork and body control, especially for post players, the biggest guys on the court. It's like high-speed ballet performed by seven-foot-tall giants holding a leather ball. Sometimes I could just lose myself in the movement and music of the game, and there more than anywhere else, I felt that sort of mind-body unity that so many reach through spiritual meditation or other means.

• • •

The fact that I loved basketball and could hold my own in most games didn't mean I always fit in on the court. I had to talk my way out of more than a couple of fistfights. It wasn't that I was trying to start shit; it was just that I knew only one way to play, the way my dad had taught me, and when I fouled someone he *knew* about it. I don't always like to admit this, but my goal when I stepped on the court was not to have fun. My goal was to *win*, and winning, coincidentally, happened to be pretty fun. But there's an important distinction there that I think pretty well defines my competitive drive.

Once I went to visit my old friend Rick in Utah, and we spent a week at a basketball camp in southern Idaho. It was held at Rick's college, a small Mormon school, and I was the only kid there who wasn't from Utah or Idaho. I was also probably the only non-Mormon in the whole camp. They just called me "Kansas," as if I was some kind of museum specimen.

Not only could you not get a drop of caffeine anywhere on campus but you could barely leave your dorm room. These were strange kids, who never cursed or farted or did anything remotely controversial. They were obedient, pious boys from good families who played sports for fun. I was a freak from the minute I arrived.

They also played a different kind of basketball than I was used to playing in Lawrence—a sterilized, sanitized, happy kind of basketball. They were friendly and sportsmanlike. They didn't talk shit or retaliate. They hadn't learned the same lessons from their fathers. They didn't knock the crap out of you when you took the ball to the basket, and they played zone defense for Chrissakes! Zone defense in a pickup game? I'd never heard of such a thing.

On top of Dad's lessons, I'd been educated in the game on the asphalt and caged courts of Lawrence, schooled in the game of Kansas *buffalo* ball, where it's every man for himself and if you aren't bleeding, you don't get a foul called. These guys in Utah had grown up playing friendly games of pickup on indoor wooden courts at their neighborhood churches. They didn't need basketball for spiritual enlightenment.

I was a blasphemous ogre tossing towheaded Mormon boys around like fragile collectible dolls and saying horrible things about their mothers. They didn't know what to do with me. Occasionally one of the coaches would say something about my language or my elbows, but they mostly avoided confronting me. Soon enough they all wanted me on their teams —mainly because they didn't want to play against me but also because I was one of the few guys over 6'3" in the whole camp. The two biggest guys were 6'8", best buddies from a small town in Idaho. They were jolly, happy kids. One of them was named Snarf and the other Studebaker.

I'm not making this up.

Of course I always had to guard one of them, and no matter how much trash I talked, how many elbows I threw, Snarf and Studebaker never got mad, never said a word, never retaliated. They seemed to be subhuman, mush-brained sponges who just smiled and congratulated me on a game well played. Not once did they threaten to kick my ass or call me a dirty name. I couldn't understand any of it. It was like we'd learned a different game. We'd definitely been raised in different basketball cultures, and I was glad to be done with that Twilight Zone experience when the week ended.

• • •

I became a much better basketball player after high school, when I didn't have to worry about impressing coaches and trying to fit into a system. I felt like those ancient Olmec hoopsters must have felt when they played in the village leagues or got together for a pickup game of Pok-ta-Pok and didn't have to worry about losing their heads.

The city leagues in Lawrence may not have been a life-and-death kind of atmosphere, but they were not for the faint of heart. Teams often recruited former college players, and the competition was fierce. Some of the best ballplayers I ever faced there never made it on a high school or college team. These guys were local playground legends, guys I'd seen at The Pit and other famous spots for pickup games. But there were also teams from local law offices and fraternities, guys not quite used to the level of play in Lawrence, who still fought hard and played dirty.

I had more than a few problems in city league and pickup games after Matt died. My anger was always right at the boiling point. I took every game a bit too seriously and played with a lot of emotion, but this is what fueled much of my competitive fire on the court and a big part of what made me successful. For a few years I wore my hair long and kept it tied back in a ponytail during games. Guys hated that. Basketball players don't wear ponytails.

I also talked a lot, trying to get in the other team's head, and there were plenty of guys who openly hated me. I could see it in a guy's face. As soon as he started paying more attention to me than to his teammates or to the ball, I knew I had him. I sometimes had crowds turn against me. The wife of a player cursed me out from the stands once when I goaded her husband into picking up his fourth and fifth fouls. I heard her shrill voice echoing in the gym, "He's cheeeeeeating. He's cheeeeating, Ref!" as her husband sat down on the bench and sulked for the rest of the game. During the postgame handshake, he cursed and threatened me with bodily harm, and as fucked up as it may sound, it made me kind of happy to see how much I had affected him.

What can I say? I needed this. If I could have worn shorts that had the words "Bye, Bye Sweetie Pie" stitched on the butt, I would have done so happily.

One time before we were married Rachel came to see one of my games at the community building downtown. I had told her how I was averaging close to a double-double in points and rebounds every game and how the team was doing well. So she came and sat in the upstairs bleachers with a few other parents, spouses, siblings, and girlfriends.

I'm not sure why I was so keyed up, but at the opening tip I said to the opposing post player, "You won't score on me."

"Oh, really," he said.

"Yeah," I said.

He just sort of chuckled and said, "Whatever, dude."

Every time he touched the ball I harassed and shoved him, blocked his shots, and even fouled him. He made a couple of free throws but didn't score a basket until the second half. I was in his face the whole time, grabbing at his arms, throwing elbows at his ribs. On offense I posted him up hard and ducked my shoulder into him on shots.

Once he came running down the court and started moving across the lane. I checked him with my forearms, and he said, "Watch the elbows, dude."

I responded with the still unexplainable "Fuck your hole" and proceeded to abuse his rib cage for the rest of the game until he got so pissed off you could see it in his face. He started missing free throws down the stretch. He barely took his eyes off me.

It was a close game at the end, and I had four fouls. I'd scored the last six points for our team and we had pulled within two. My teammate threw me the ball as I was running down the sideline, and this guy, a little guard I'd also been abusing all through the game, stepped in front of me as my head was turned to catch the ball. I took one step and plowed into him forty feet from the basket. The guy went down in a heap and yelled like he was hurt. It was a sucker flop, but the ref blew his whistle and called me for my fifth foul.

I don't know quite what happened, but something snapped inside me and I just exploded. I starting screaming at the other player, pointing my finger and yelling, "You fucking pussy. That's such a bullshit move. You know you can't stop me, so you fucking flop. You're a pussy and you suck."

The ref blew his whistle again and jerked his thumb toward the exit. "You're out of here, buddy," he said.

I stormed off the court, still fuming and spewing curse words. My coach was bitching at the refs too as I gathered my stuff and headed for the exit. As I was leaving, I unleashed another tirade of expletives at the guy until the refs started moving in my direction and pointing toward the door. I looked up and saw Rachel sitting there in the bleachers, watching the whole thing. I'd forgotten she was there, and I wanted to run and hide. She met me in the lobby, and I could tell she didn't really know what to say. She was a little bit afraid of what she'd witnessed.

"I'm sorry, Steve," she said and rubbed her hand on my shoulder. "I'm really sorry."

Then she left, and we drove to our separate houses in our separate cars.

I didn't have many outlets for my anger. It was little things—missing keys, traffic, getting dressed—that would set me off most times. Basketball seemed to help. It kept me afloat. It was a release, something else to focus my attention and aggression, and it gave me an unbelievable adrenaline rush—even if I wasn't always embraced by those around me, even if I was scared of myself sometimes.

• • •

Although I don't play much basketball anymore, I still consider myself a rabid fan. I have an encyclopedic knowledge of basketball trivia and can recall things about players and teams and games that nobody else cares about. In the academic world, the world of arts, my love for basketball can be something that sets me apart and makes me feel a bit freakish.

My artist and writer friends aren't sure what to make of me when I start talking basketball. Their eyes just glass over, and they smile and nod as if I'm speaking a foreign language.

Sometimes they'll ask me if I'm serious—sort of like they do when I start talking about the *Guinness Book of World Records*. Of course I'm serious. Dead serious. But I guess that's the nature of obsession. It necessarily sets you apart. If it wasn't unique and a bit alienating, it wouldn't be an obsession. It would be more like a hobby or a pastime.

After I applied to Ph.D. programs in philosophy, a university in California paid for me to fly there and tour the campus. I still hadn't decided for sure if I wanted to pursue graduate work, but I came along with several other candidates, not quite realizing that it was something of an audition for spots—or at least for funding. I was expected to be on my best behavior and show off all my intelligence. I was supposed to wow them with my recall of the history of philosophy and impress them with my vision for future projects in the study of ethical theory.

One problem was that the visit happened to coincide with March Madness, the NCAA men's basketball tournament. I was in California for two games involving my alma mater and favorite team, the Kansas Jayhawks. The other problem was that Rachel was back home in Kansas. She had another year of school left and wouldn't be coming with me to California or Connecticut or wherever I decided to pursue my Ph.D. She would be staying home.

I was supposed to be imagining myself in this place, trying it on for size, and they had me rooming with three seriously dorky grad students who talked about nothing but philosophy and made inside jokes about Wittgenstein that I pretended to get. They didn't have a television, and they looked at me like I was deranged when I asked if they were basketball fans. My second night there I was scheduled to attend a party at the department chair's house. Of course, the party happened to coincide with one of the Jayhawks' games.

I was doomed from the beginning.

I tried to mingle and schmooze for a while, but (this may come as a shock to hear) philosophers are *boring*. I just couldn't take it anymore and quietly slipped away into a back bedroom, where I found the department chair's ten-year-old son watching the game. I sat down next to him on the edge of the bed.

"Mind if I watch?" I asked.

"Sure," he said.

"You like the Jayhawks?"

"Yeah, but Stanford is my favorite," he said.

"Montgomery is a great coach," I said. "Love their guards."

"You one of the students?" he asked, gesturing toward the door and the party beyond. We had the volume down low so we wouldn't disturb the grown-ups.

"I doubt it," I said and left it at that.

I don't know how long I was there, but it must have been a while, because the department chair came looking for me. When he opened the door and saw me sitting there with his son watching basketball, the puzzled and disappointed look on his face told me there was no way in hell they would offer me any kind of financial assistance to study there, and I'd be lucky even to get an offer of admission. My fate was sealed.

The truth was I didn't care. The Jayhawks won. I got to see the game, and I made a new ten-year-old friend who was blissfully ignorant of Wittgenstein, someone who would probably have been more interested in the Guinness Books than in the Great Books. I'd do the same thing all over again. You have to be willing to sacrifice something for your obsessions, and at the time a Ph.D. for a basketball game seemed like a pretty good trade.

• • •

I needed a break from philosophy. I'd been enrolled in several graduate-level courses in things like ethical theory, epistemology, metaphysics, and the philosophy of law, because the department allowed their high-achieving undergraduate students to take them and they had seemed like fun. But the work had nearly killed me. My brain was tired. I needed an escape from the analytical dissection of texts, a break from having to read something four times just to figure out what the hell the author was trying to say.

So I was happy when during the first meeting of my first writing class, the teacher walked in and told everyone that we had a story due in two weeks. I'd never written a story in my life, but I poured myself into the assignment and handed it in ahead of the deadline. When we showed up for class, the teacher had picked my story for discussion and invited me to read it out loud. I'd never spoken in front of this many people, certainly never read anything I'd written in public, but I walked up there and sat down on a table.

I looked up to see forty or fifty pairs of eyes staring at me. I looked back down at my story and started to read. The teacher stopped me once to tell me to slow down, and I tried to concentrate on speaking slowly and carefully as I kept reading. My story was an autobiographical narrative about a college student who loses his brother in a car accident and, overwhelmed with grief and anger at the world, climbs up on the roof of a campus building with a high-powered rifle.

Subtle, huh?

It gets better.

The narrator is blind without his Coke-bottle-thick glasses and removes them before he begins taking potshots at oak trees and street signs. The poor kid doesn't actually want to hurt someone. It's all very dramatic and tragic. While I read, the teacher sat at the back of the class and took notes. He wore this light blue and white striped suit and looked like an old-time tonic salesman or carnival barker. He sort of smiled at me when I looked up, as if he was enjoying it, and this helped. He seemed to know how much I needed this, seemed to know this was more than a story to me.

The rest of the class was pitched forward in their seats, gawking at me. So I kept reading, finally settling into a consistent pace and voice. I was telling them how the narrator has trouble communicating his feelings to his girlfriend, and even though I was talking about myself, the story ceased to be *about* me. It was about that kid with the gun on the roof and his glasses clutched in his fist, the kid who lost his brother and doesn't know how to deal with it but he's trying to find some way to express himself, some way to fit into the new world.

At one point in the story, the kid sights down the barrel at a young woman walking across campus, pulls the trigger, and just barely misses her head, splintering a tree nearby. As I read this most dramatic moment, a woman in the class gasped audibly, sucking in a quick breath of air, an involuntary little seal

173

bark of emotion. It was a raw and beautiful sound I will never forget.

I paused for a second to register this reaction to my words, and a feeling moved through me like a shot of painkiller, followed by a jolt of electricity. I looked around, and the class was riveted, staring up at me with rapt attention as I kept reading. The story concludes with police storming the roof and shooting our narrator when he raises his gun and points it at them.

The story was pretty awful—juvenile and melodramatic and sensational. But it was honest—perhaps painfully so— and that woman's gasp was so seductive, so addictive, I knew there was no turning back. I finished my philosophy degree but knew that I had opened a door I couldn't close up again. I had caused a woman to gasp, just with something I wrote, a few sentences and paragraphs cobbled together into a thinly veiled autobiographical story about my brother and me. I had created drama, manufactured emotion—sort of like I'd done with my class journal so many years ago—but this time it felt bigger, heavier, more important.

Home Runs.

Henry L. (Hank) Aaron broke the major league record set by George H. (Babe) Ruth of 714 home runs in a lifetime when he hit No. 715 on April 8, 1974. Between 1954 and 1974 he hit 733 home runs in the National League. In 1975, he switched over to the American League and in that year and 1976, when he finally retired, he hit 22 more, bringing his lifetime total to 755, the major league record. (1980, 515)

Hero, Home Run.

When Henry Aaron smacked home run number 715 over the wall, I was just two years old—roughly the same age my son is now. Though I didn't see the record-breaking hit live, I've watched it over and over again in televised replays—believing that it belonged in the pantheon of Great Sports Moments I kept cataloged in my head.

I know you've seen the film footage that I've seen, those pictures promising a moment of pure joy. As the ball clears the outfield wall, two impulsive fans drop to the evergreen field and run after Hank. Accompanying the picture is the roar of a crowd erupting into a frenzy, the drop of jaws, the drop of drinks and hot dogs, the positively religious exaltation.

This one white fan—his wild hair flying and his toothy mouth smiling—he's the first one there. He jumps from his seat. Legs pumping, he gallops for the infield. Hank trots around the bases, waving to the crowd. He's just knocked the Babe from his throne. He doesn't see the guy coming.

To me, the fan is this loose-limbed image of unadulterated happiness—or at least that's what I thought, that's what I believed. As a child of pop culture, I had learned to trust the promises of television and technology.

> *Jesus loves me, this I know.*
> *Because the TV tells me so.*

I figured this fan must have seen the home run before it even left Hank's bat, right in mid-swing. He saw the swipe of the stick, the path of the ball—and he knew Ruth's record was gone. I imagine he'd been following the record march, chalking up dingers on his wall at home, maybe scratching them into the back of his bedroom door with a jackknife his father gave him for his fifth birthday.

He could be nineteen years old, still living in his mother's basement. For a ticket to the game, maybe he sold his most prized possession—a miniature bicycle built for him by his Chinese neighbor— the World's Smallest Bicycle. Maybe he loved this bicycle, with its tiny rubber-band tires, spokes made from copper wire, and a frame bent from a clothes hanger. The crank was carved from a bottle cap, and the pedals actually worked. It must have hurt him deeply to watch it go.

Perhaps he understood the importance of sacrifice.

Maybe this boy and his neighbor had watched Hank Saturdays on television when his mother was working at the church. He taught her new English words like *strike, ball, bullpen, fastball, slider.* She taught him the secret of silence between notes and, in her happiest moments, the trick to dancing with houseflies. Perhaps he was a boy searching for something and he'd read about Jay Gwaltney in the Guinness Books, telling his parents over dinner one night that he planned to eat the fifteen-foot evergreen in the backyard.

As an alternative, perhaps his mother paid their eccentric neighbor for piano lessons. She was supposed to be his teacher, but she sat close to him on the bench while he practiced, her hand on his leg, her finger reading the inseam of his jeans. The mother had no idea. The teacher whispered the play-by-play from Hank Aaron's baseball games. Because she did not own a television at first, she whispered words she had memorized from game-day recordings he slipped into her mailbox after dark. "Aaron steps up to the plate. The two-two pitch. He swings. And, oh baby, it's outta here."

She made miniature toys she could have sold to emperors—boats, cars, trains, and trucks—all from scrap metal. She built the World's Smallest Tandem Bicycle too. She told stories with her hands fluttering around her face. But now . . . she knew when he skipped his lesson one day that his mother had found out about them. He left her arms years ago, but now she sees him on the television she purchased, and he has pushed his way up to the wall, waiting for the hard crack of Hank's bat to ball. She sees him there, all tanned and handsome, and wonders, what about the bicycle between them? But something inside tells her it is all gone.

There was nothing musical about his leaving, because he always loved Henry Aaron—probably more than he loved her. He would have given anything for this moment, even the World's Smallest Bicycle, and she had to understand this better than I could ever imagine. Maybe as I did, this white boy dreamed often of black heroes. Maybe he never practiced his piano at home, but instead read biographies of athletes, and obsessed over the details of their lives. He probably hated playing the game of baseball, even trembled when he stood at the plate, terrified at the thought of another kid chucking a hard leather ball at his head. Maybe it's because Hank's story—like all these stories—is a story of overcoming great adversity, and everyone loves those stories. This boy's mother probably didn't understand why it was so important. She never knew a thing of

Babe Ruth, the white giant. She sat at home reluctantly tuning her radio to the game.

Maybe all of this would make a difference if it were true. But it's not.

Whatever the reason, whatever he left behind to be there, this man sees Hank's winning swing. He has a jump on the ball—as if he knew it was coming—and runs hard to catch Hank between second and third base. Hank just trots around the diamond, waving to the crowd, not gloating about it. That's not his way. But then this guy bursts into the picture and slaps Hank hard on the back. Hank turns at the last second—I like to imagine that the fan calls him "Mr. Aaron"—and says something beautiful, something to fit the image given me by the television cameras. This guy just seems so happy, so proud, but I don't honestly know what he's thinking.

Thanks again to television, I *do* know now what Hank was thinking at the moment. I watched a special on the 50 Greatest Televised Moments in Sports, and they included this footage of Hank's home run. I don't remember where it ranked, but they interviewed him, and it was the first time I'd heard him talk about the context of that record-setting home run. Hank sat there, looking healthy and handsome, and he talked about how what should have been his proudest moment had already been soiled by repeated phone calls to his home, threats whispered into the receiver, threats against his children filled with racial epithets. I couldn't believe what I was hearing. I wanted to crawl inside the television and start yanking out circuits and fuses until I found the one responsible. I wanted to pick apart these images and build them back into something different.

I can admit that I love television—or at least what TV promises—but I know I have to teach my son not to trust it.

I believed that this young man in the film footage, stupid with joy, his limbs all loose in the rush of pride, just wanted to share Hank's triumph—as if he was saying for all of us, "You are the World's Greatest, a World Record Holder." But Hank admitted that in the heat of that moment—just for a split second—he believed the guy had come there to kill him, put a bullet in his head right there on the field in front of his teammates and the world. I heard Hank say this, and suddenly it came rushing back. Of course I remember reading about this, but that image from the TV held such sway over me, I couldn't get past the surface.

When I heard Hank's words some thirty years later, I saw this moment through different eyes, saw parts of my childhood through different eyes. I realized again the false promises of television. Outside of my dad and my brother, so many of my heroes seemed to be paper and celluloid heroes, only half real and partially true. I don't know why it surprised me when they didn't live up to my imagination.

I felt this overwhelming urge to apologize to Hank Aaron for this less than heroic fan—for his grin, his gait, his slap, and for the 1974 world of which I was just barely conscious, for which I was just barely responsible. I wanted to apologize for this man's dreams, his skin color, my skin color, and my innocent belief. I felt like a sucker, and I wanted to think my words could make a difference. I wanted to apologize to his imaginary Chinese lover and her World Record Bicycles, apologize because the word sort of rhymes with *lies* and I don't know what else to say.

Fastest Amputation.

The shortest time recorded for the amputation of a leg in the pre-anesthetic era was 13 to 15 seconds by Napoleon's chief surgeon, Dominique Larrey. There could have been no ligation.* (1980, 49)

Bed of Nails.

The duration record for non-stop lying on a bed of nails (sharp 6-inch nails 2 inches apart) is 65 hours 43 minutes 21 seconds by Tim Robinson (Strombo the Maniac) at Oval House Theatre Club, London, on June 16–19, 1977. Much longer durations are claimed by uninvigilated *fakirs*** —the most extreme case being *Silki* who claimed 111 days in São Paulo, Brazil, ending on August 24, 1969. (1980, 453)

From *Merriam-Webster's Ninth New Collegiate Dictionary: Ligation* n. 1: an act of ligating 2: something that binds. *Ligature* n. 1:a: Something that is used to bind; specif: a filament (as a thread) used in surgery.

From *Merriam Webster's Ninth New Collegiate Dictionary: Fakir* n. 1.a: Muslim mendicant: DERVISH b: an itinerant Hindu ascetic or wonder-worker 2. IMPOSTOR: esp: swindler.

Scars, Most, on Right Side of Body.

There's a picture out there of someone like me. He has the same brown hair, same brown eyes, same lips and fleshy saucers for ears. He looks exactly like me. But it's not me, not really.

He's an impostor.

I had the photo taken during my senior year in high school, just like all the other kids. But the final product shows the unblemished face of a different boy, an All-American boy I barely recognize. I remember signing a disclaimer for the photographer—something about them touching up unsightly scars and blemishes—but the information never sunk in, never seemed to refer to *my* face in any way.

I posed in his wood-paneled basement, his green yard full of faux fences and photogenic trees. I wore a striped rugby shirt, propped my arm up on a wagon wheel, and smiled until my cheeks ached from the effort. When we received the pictures, the large scar on my right cheek, the one I've had most of my life and become rather attached to, had been airbrushed out, completely erased from my face.

I didn't realize they'd be touching up my identity.

The picture spread through the family like an ugly rumor, making its way onto other walls, into wallets, photo albums, and the Lawrence High School yearbook.

· · ·

Many friends have told me that they never notice my scar. I've even had some ask if it was the result of a recent accident, claiming never to have seen the marks before that moment. But other people tell me it's the first thing they notice. Some have said it makes me look tough or intimidating, even sexy and mysterious. People have assumed that I have a violent past, or that I earned my scar in hand-to-hand combat of some kind.

A friend who was recently discharged from the Army told me that his fellow soldiers would have paid money to have a scar like mine. "It would have earned you some serious points," he said.

Perhaps I make too much of it, just like I do my size. As a man, I realize I'm not expected to be openly self-conscious about my appearance. But it takes only one person, one comment, to spin me off again.

At work recently an older woman, a so-called nontraditional student, sat down in a chair next to my desk and asked for my help. I began filling out the requisite forms, and out of the blue she said, "That's a hell of a scar on your face."

I was stunned. "Yeah, sixteen stitches," I said.

"You look like a pirate," she said. "You should wear an eye patch."

An awkward, gassy silence settled over the room.

An eye patch? How do you respond to that? I said something about having the scar most of my life, and my voice just sort of trailed off as I focused my attention on the computer screen.

"Wow, you've lived that whole time looking like a pirate," she persisted.

"Yep," I said, "and I never dressed up as one for Halloween.

How about that?" This time I let my sarcasm slip out a little, and I think she sensed it.

"I have two boys, you know," she said. "They were always getting hurt." She said this as if it somehow granted her the right to make comments about my face.

"Dressed up as Frankenstein once," I said. "You know, with corks glued to my neck like bolts." This was true. Third grade, I think. "They kept falling off and I'd have to stick them back." I'd also dressed up as the Grim Reaper. I was a jolly kid.

She asked if I painted stitch marks on my scar. I told her that I did, and we both just sat there staring at each other.

I wanted to tell her that she looked like John Denver with boobs—same haircut, same goofy grin and glasses—but I didn't say a word. That would be rude. That would be unprofessional. I really didn't know what to say to her. I wondered whether if I had a goiter she would've made some comment about that: "Jesus, it looks like you swallowed a football."

I get this sort of thing more with my size. For some reason it's socially acceptable for total strangers to call me "Big Guy," when I'd never refer to a small man as "Little Guy," or an obviously obese person as "Fat Guy." But nobody ever called me "Scarface" or "Pirate Steve"—at least not until this woman showed up in my office.

She left that day and I knew I'd probably never see her again, but I can't get her words out of my head. "You look like a pirate." Could I be a swashbuckling marauder, a scar-faced sea captain who rapes and pillages? Could I be that big, bad, and scary?

Sure it seems silly. But still to this day I tell stories about the woman who said I looked like a pirate. Everyone laughs, but the truth is I probably would never remember that incident if I hadn't already been a little self-conscious about my scar. It wouldn't have been funny if it didn't hurt just a little bit.

. . .

After my son was born, the nurse in the special care unit asked if I wanted to keep the paper scrub jumpsuit I was wearing— perhaps as some kind of memento or trophy. They had demanded that I wear this thing, even though it didn't come anywhere close to fitting me, and as soon as I pulled it on, the crotch and the armpits blew out into wide splits. Who do they make these for anyway? The arms barely reached past my elbows and the legs barely past my knees. They gave me paper booties and told me to put them over my shoes. I couldn't even get them over my toes, so I went skating down the hospital halls in socks and blue booties, the pant legs bunched up around my knees like I was MC Hammer.

Unlike a lot of families these days, we don't have any pictures of Malcolm's birth. No videos. No Polaroids. No digital photos saved on the computer. But what are we really missing? There aren't a lot of images to share with others when you go through a cesarean section. Rachel has a scar to show for it, a memento of her own, and I always have my imagination to fill the gaps.

So I turned down the nurse's offer to keep the gown, ripped it off, and deposited it in the trash bin. But ever since then— and maybe because *she* attached some value to it—I have told stories about the jumpsuit and paper booties, describing how silly I looked, and wished that I had taken the nurse's offer and stashed the scrubs somewhere for safekeeping.

I guess there's a big part of me that likes feeling too big for normal-size things, part of me that revels in the attention. It's probably good I didn't keep the scrubs. I'd pull them out for dinner guests or glue swaths of the fabric into photo albums. I'd tell stories about that day and make it sound like I was the Incredible Hulk bursting out of my clothes to catch my son as he emerged from the womb. But the truth is I felt a whole lot less heroic and virile, especially when they wheeled Rachel into the operating room for prep and I was left alone in the hall wearing my tattered blue paper gown and silly hat.

• • •

As a kid I loved the Incredible Hulk, in both the comic book and the TV show, even if he did give me nightmares. I identified with his size, his loneliness, and his anger—and that piano music at the end of the show was always so very, very sad. Probably to a lot of other kids, my appreciation for the Hulk was obvious. I *was* the Hulk—big, sullen, and socially awkward.

I had a reputation at Hillcrest Elementary as a bully, but I don't remember feeling like one. I wasn't a bad person. At least that's not how I imagined myself most of the time—even if I *had* pulled a knife on my best friend when we were in kindergarten, even if Matt would certainly have lumped me into the category. But I didn't pick on Matt so much physically as psychologically. I'd twist his words around and point out errors in his logic, telling him repeatedly that he made no sense, playing mind games with him. It's no wonder he once hauled off and kicked me in the head. Matt wasn't completely innocent either. We both played our parts, the way brothers always do.

I didn't seek out the bully identity, and I'm still a little defensive about it. I thought I was playing the same games, doing the same things that other boys were doing. It was just that they were half my size and all pink-skinned and weak and innocent looking; and when I tackled someone on the playground, or called people names, the teachers said it was different.

Once or twice kids made the mistake of calling me "Scarface," and my vengeance came swiftly and violently. I socked Jeff Farmer in the gut for it, and he doubled over, the wind knocked out of him, gasping for breath, until the teacher came running. That's the way it usually worked. I reacted and people got hurt.

The truth was I kind of liked the nickname "Scarface." It had a lot more playground credibility than "Lurch" and sounded pretty cool. What I didn't like was that I had been singled out and targeted for teasing because of it. I wanted to be part of the crowd, one of the boys doing the pointing and taunting. At least I thought that's what I wanted.

Then Amjad came along. His family had moved here from Pakistan, and his father was teaching at the university. Our school had a lot of the kids of faculty and graduate students, kids like Amjad, but he was different somehow. He was a noisy loner, a misanthrope with puckish characteristics. Rather than try to fit in, he broke rules and caused trouble and seemed oblivious to any censure from teachers. Even the sharpest verbal arrows from peers bounced off of him.

Nobody could figure out if Amjad was terribly smart or terribly stupid, but he often set himself up for teasing by violating childhood protocol and crossing lines other kids were afraid to approach. There was a freedom to his actions that we envied. He butted in line and left his seat regularly. He didn't keep his hands to himself. He played games at recess for which he didn't know the rules and didn't care when he broke them.

He wore black dress socks with brown sandals.

He wasn't like the other children, and for whatever reason, Sam Flock and I took it upon ourselves to taunt and tease Amjad into submission. Sam would borrow one of his Crayolas, break it in half, then piece it back together so that when Amjad picked it up, it would fall apart in his hand. I would wait until we were in crowds together—maybe in line for lunch or the drinking fountain—then pinch Amjad in the ribs and pretend nothing had happened. He would look around accusingly, make a strange face, and scamper down the hall. He didn't cry or throw fits or go tattling to the teacher. He seemed to take it all quite well.

Then one day Sam and I got called to the principal's office. Amjad hadn't been at school the last couple of days and his father had called. Amjad wasn't sleeping at night. He'd been having nightmares about Sam and me. He was afraid to sleep, worried we would visit him in his dreams, and terrified of going to school.

I was dumbfounded and traumatized. Both Sam and I were. Sam's family were Christian Scientists, and though I wasn't really sure what this meant, I knew his mother would be as horrified as mine was.

We just didn't think we were causing damage like that. It seemed like normal boy behavior, not the intentional product of some warped psyches. Yes, it was cruel, but I recognize that only in retrospect. At the time it felt as innocent as any other teasing and taunting that seemed to define most male interactions at that age.

Sure Sam and I were the biggest boys in the school, probably as big as Amjad's parents. We were bruising, intelligent children, testing out the roles of manhood, participating in all the rituals. I felt stupid for not seeing the consequences, not seeing the effects of our actions, and I was racked with guilt for years. In fact I'm still struggling to accept that I gave someone nightmares much like the Incredible Hulk had tormented me, and that I did it unintentionally, without really thinking about it. I like to believe there's always a good reason for the choices I make and the impression I have on others, but it's just not that easy.

· · ·

I think the only way I could set a Guinness Record is if it was for something completely unintentional or involuntary, something glandular, hormonal, or accidental. I've tried to think of things that might qualify me as Guinness-worthy. Barring a sudden and massive weight gain, this list is the best I can come up with:

Scars, Most, on Right Side of Body Alone. **Steven Church, 32, of Fort Collins, Colorado. Twelve scars (surgical repair from injury, deep cuts or punctures, and burns only), total of 68 stitches (see list below in order from toe to head). The noticeable absence of scars or significant wounds on the left side of Mr. Church's body makes this entry unique. A scar on his right cheek once prompted the remark "You look like a pirate."**

Puncture Wounds (two). **Shin. Caused by bicycle chain ring. Resembles bite mark.**

Puncture Wound + Rip. **Twelve stitches surface, six interior stitches. Inside right calf. Resulting from drunken fall from landscaping retaining wall, catching leg on exposed steel rebar.**

Discolored Skin. **Kneecap. Scar tissue from bicycle accident on sandstone. (See also elbow and shoulder below.) Moab, Utah.**

Surgical Scar. **Knee. 24 + 6 stitches. Repair of anterior cruciate tear with patellar reconstruction.**

Burn. **Inside thigh. Second to third degree. Roughly 1 inch wide and 3 inches long. Resulted from inappropriate contact with motorcycle tailpipe.**

Knife Wound. **Thumb pad. 1 1/2 inches long. Accident in kitchen store. Runs from tip almost to first knuckle.**

Burn. **Inside forearm, otherwise known as the "fish belly." Exhaust burn from gas-powered mower.**

Discolored Skin. **Elbow. Scar tissue from bicycle accident on sandstone. (See knee above and shoulder below.)**

Split. **Chin. Four stitches required to close wound caused by aggressive Jet Ski maneuvers.**

Crescent Scar. Cheek. Twelve stitches. Resulted from confrontation with aluminum guide track for garage door.

Crease. Eyebrow. Four stitches. Resulted from confrontation with aluminum guide track (see above).

Of course I realize that there are thousands of people who, with one major surgery, have topped my stitch total and even tripled it. But that's not the point. I've become attached to my scars— sort of like I've become attached to the Guinness characters—mainly because of the stories they tell, the memories they hold, the records they keep.

I've tried to make up stories for the origins of my facial scars, even convincing myself that I need to have a couple of stock stories on hand I can drop on unsuspecting strangers, anecdotes that seem to fit their expectations, but it's difficult to do. It's sort of like trying to make up a convincing story for the origin of your ears. They're part of you and they always have been. That's it.

• • •

Because I've grown so comfortable with my scars, it does surprise and unnerve me every time I see that picture of a boy like me—that fresh-faced, clean-cheeked young man—in my parents' house. It's a strange kind of "out-of-body" experience. Because he's a different boy, someone else's son, and I wonder how he has risen to such prominence in their lives. I wonder how he has become so cherished, so honored as to have a nine-by-twelve framed photograph on the wall.

He *is* a little better looking than I am. There is no jagged line curling up from the edge of his smile almost to his eye, no thin, four-stitch stripe hidden in the eyebrow. He looks like a son you could be proud to call your own. Ask him to squint and you won't see where he flinched before the impact and probably saved his eye. Neighbors never told his mother that she's lucky he's no girl. The ER doctor never called them "bad parents" for putting their four-year-old on a bicycle.

I still wouldn't want his face. I've grown attached to my scar like most people become attached to the curves of their noses, the dangles of their earlobes, the color of their eyes. It's like a tattoo I didn't pick off the wall, a rough sketch of split seconds from my childhood memory, a true original. My scar marks time for me: Year of the Face comes before others—Year of the Burn, Year of the Knee, Year of the Brother. To me, the real blemish in my parents' pictures is my clean, pink cheek, empty of stories, empty of identity. If anything, they should be touching up photos by adding scars. But what I see is not what they see, not what a stranger sees. My face is not entirely my own. It's something I put out there, a vanity text given to others to read and interpret. Some people prefer a blank slate. I know this now. Look closely. Do you see my happiness? Do you see something else? Tell me. I have ears like satellite dishes. I can take it.

• • •

I've tried to find good reasons why all of my stitches, every one of my serious injuries, have afflicted only the right half of my body. I wonder if it has something to do with the whole right brain-left brain distinction.

My left hand is basically useless, barely able to handle a basketball or hold a pencil; and then there's my history of childhood seizures and sinus infections, combined with recent bouts of meningitis and West Nile—both of them mosquito-borne brain viruses. So I can't help but think that all of these disorders are evidence of some fundamental defect, a serious disconnect between brain and body, a structural fault, or lack of cooperation between the right side and the left side that results in clumsiness, oafishness, or a simple tendency to fall to the right. This conclusion seems correct to me and explains something I've felt all along—that my body has an identity of its own, a life independent of my intentions, dreams, and desires.

Recently while I was getting a massage, the woman told me that the right side of my body is heavier than my left side. She stood with her hands on my feet, practicing some Reiki energy work that all seemed a bit hokey to me until she started talking about the difference between the "hemispheres" of my body. When she tried to move the energy through my legs, something strange happened.

As she moved down the right side, pressing her hands into my hips and shoulders, I could feel things start to loosen. When she asked if I'd experienced any deep loss, I mentioned my brother's death and felt my whole body snap like a rubber band and go limp.

"Did you feel that?" she asked.

"Yeah, that was weird."

"You're carrying a lot of grief on your right side," she said. "You have to let it go, let it move."

. . .

Most people I meet don't ask about the scars on my face. Children are usually the exceptions. They often ask with the first question out of their mouths—and I don't mind telling them. A boy stares up at my face, and his eyes will have this glow of freedom, where *right* and *wrong* are fuzzy dots in his field of vision, just words his parents toss around in the air. Nobody censors his curiosity.

He asks, "What happened to your face?"

Someday Malcolm will ask me the same. The question doesn't really bother me, but sometimes the kid's eyes fade with disappointment when I tell him what actually happened. I can see that the stories he has already imagined are much more interesting than the truth. A bike wreck just isn't that exciting. He sees knife fight, street fight, fistfight; or maybe a rock-climbing injury, a hang-gliding wound, a drag-racing accident. He sees a hero or a pirate. He sees adventure—secret agent, James Bond, Dirty Harry kind of adventure. It seems easy to follow the tracks, to trace the stitches back to some steam engine of a story that can pull a lot of weight. But he sees something else in my face—what you might call "character," this long train of stories behind my face, lined up like boxcars from past to present.

But what kind of character? What kind of person will Malcolm see in my face? Movies are marked with faces like mine—scarred up to show some deep-seated darkness of character. Think of Al Pacino as Tony Montana in *Scarface* —the ripples rolling out from images of Al Capone, the most famous scar-faced mobster. Think of Tom Berenger in *Pla-*

toon, the sadistic sergeant who has spent too long in the jungle to know right from wrong. His face is a map of scars. He kills women and children, and I bet when he was a boy he teased other kids until they had nightmares.

These men carry their scars like trophies too. But trophies for what? Their capability for violence? Their embrace of the dark side? When these men were boys, they probably pulled knives on their best friends. They probably bullied their siblings too. They seem to live up to the promises of their scars.

I can admit that there are times when I enjoy these sorts of dark and violent associations. I play it up—wearing my hair buzzed short, black clothes, and an earring in each of my ears. I furrow my brow when strangers stare in bars. I swagger up and down the basketball court in pickup games, letting my tongue wag, pushing and shoving in the paint. But the truth is I've never been much of a fighter, always been more frightened than fearless. All my surface wounds are self-inflicted, most of my scars trophies to the violence of chance.

• • •

I imagine that everyone sees my scars right away and wonders about the story behind them. I assume people might even make up their own stories. I've even done it myself to a girl who worked in the library on campus. She had more scars than I do—big ones that curled up from her lip and carved through her chin and cheek.

I found myself wondering about the origins, making up stories about car wrecks on prom night, plate-glass windows, or a dog mauling when she was just a girl—speculating in the same way I accuse others of doing. Was I wrong? Perhaps. Yet I still found myself looking for this girl every time I visited the library, trying to catch a glimpse of her scars across the rows of computers. But she always disappeared before I had the courage to ask for the stories in her face.

• • •

I once met a semi-famous Czech novelist and screenwriter on a cold Friday in November. I'd been asked to drive him from his hotel to the university for a discussion with students. Before he had even arrived, the community buzzed with whispers of his dynamic personality. Phone conversations were quoted for effect.

So I was excited and a little nervous as I drove to the hotel and parked out front. After I called his room and waited for a few minutes, he greeted me in the lobby.

"Hello," he said, shaking my hand and placing his other hand on my arm, as if he was transmitting more than words. "You are Steven."

"Yes," I said, and he paused for a moment or two, looking up at me to register my height.

He was a wrinkled man in his seventies with silver hair, but his face was that of a child—jeweled with urgently curious eyes that fix themselves on you and won't let go. He possessed a certain energy like the traction beam of some vessel from another galaxy. Every line of his face—from eyes to lips to chin —seemed to point up until his whole face smiled.

He followed me to my car, and we talked casually about the weather. He said he loved the cold here. I waited for the connection, for something deeper that I'd heard was his way—not this small talk I was accustomed to with most people.

Perhaps I was being selfish, asking for more than I deserved. After all, we had just met. But how often does someone get the chance to spend time with a semi-famous novelist and screenwriter, a survivor of three Nazi death camps, a man who has lived through horrors I couldn't presume to imagine? He'd barely said a word and I was already in awe.

He sat down in the passenger seat next to me and asked without hesitation. "How did you get your scar?" He drew his finger across his cheek and pointed at mine.

He posed his question with the same innocence and aplomb that children often do. If I wasn't expecting some shrugging of social norms from him, I might have been surprised by his candor. But this was the connection I'd been expecting, that deeper level of discourse for which I'd been waiting. Excited for the opportunity, I began to explain that the scar came from a bicycle accident when I was four years old.

He cut me off mid-sentence. "It wasn't with the swords?" He made a swishing sword motion in the air with his finger. He had a very serious look on his face. I was confused.

"No," I said, "not from the swords."

He explained that a facial scar like mine is a sign of German aristocracy—something boys earn in military academy sword fights. It's a badge of honor on the flesh, something that sets one apart.

"The Germans would love you," he said.

What I wanted to say was, "I didn't earn anything. I simply fell into this face. I didn't try to give myself a scar." I could have said, "The past is the past," but it wouldn't have been true. And suddenly I wanted desperately to be that fresh-faced boy from my parents' pictures—with his easy smile, his casual lean, his rugby shirt and clean, pink cheek, empty of scars, empty of identity. I wished I'd had the face of an All-American football hero, a fisherman, a carpenter, or a friendly janitor—someone generic and nonthreatening, anything but a German military man. I wished I could disappear into some other skin or just wash my scar away with a long shower, some harsh soap, and a scouring pad.

Egg Drop.

The greatest height from
which fresh eggs landed without
breaking was from 600 feet from a
helicopter by [*sic*] David S. Donoghue and
John Cartwright, on February 8, 1974. (1980, 462)

Parachute, Longest Fall
Without Parachute.

The greatest altitude from which anyone has bailed out without a parachute and survived is 21,980 feet. This occurred in
January, 1942, when Lt. (now Lt.-Col.) I. M. Chisov (U.S.S.R.)
fell from an Ilyushin 4 which had been severely damaged.
He struck the ground a glancing blow on the edge of a
snow-covered ravine and slid to the bottom. (1980, 475)

Fall, Hardest.

During one of the last winters that Rachel and I were child-less and relatively carefree, we invited some of her friends to join us for a ski weekend in Winter Park at my family's cabin. At our urging, they brought Jason, their rambunctious seven-year-old.

Our first night there it was cold—the kind of temperature that freezes the moisture in your nose—and we were walking back to the house after a pleasant meal at the local overpriced Cajun restaurant. We'd all had a little wine and were feeling good.

Jason's dad and mom were walking ahead, talking with Rachel, while I lingered back with Jason. He grabbed my arm and hung there while I walked and dragged him down the side-walk. I started swinging my arm a bit, and he liked that, letting out squeals and whoops, his little voice piercing the night.

"More! More! More!" he demanded, and I dangled my hand out like a fishing lure.

He stopped, took a couple of running steps, grabbed my arm, and swung hard, kicking his legs up in the air. He rose up off the pavement and seemed to take my arm with him.

I grabbed at his coat, but my hand slipped.

I clutched at his mitten, but it came off in my grip.

Jason's little body floated in the air for a second, suspended between his parents and me, before crashing to the sidewalk.

His head bounced off the icy concrete with a loud *crack,* and the sound of it seemed to reverberate through the cold air, ricocheting off the buildings and cars, and finally fracturing something deep inside me.

When he complained of ringing in his ears, his parents took Jason to the emergency room. As they were walking out the cabin door, Jason peeked over his dad's shoulder and grinned at us. It was a sly, mischievous grin. The doctors checked him out and just sent them back, telling them to look for signs of concussion. The panic passed, and we had a good time for the next couple of days.

Jason showed no ill effects from his fall, but I still felt horribly guilty. I found myself avoiding him for the rest of the weekend and sort of retreated into myself for a while. Even though I knew it wasn't all my fault or all Jason's fault, and that "fault" didn't really matter, I couldn't seem to get over it. The sound of his head cracking on the pavement just stayed with me.

Rachel and I had been talking about having kids—maybe seriously for the first time—and I was starting to imagine myself as a father. I liked the idea of being a playmate, even a jungle gym, for my own kid, but when I dropped Jason on his head, I began to question if I'd ever be ready for that kind of responsibility. I wasn't sure I could handle being a dad, the mature one who keeps his cool and doesn't panic. I reassured myself by saying that kids are resilient, that injuries and danger are just a matter of life, and you get through them.

It's a few months later, springtime in Colorado, and we've been invited over to Jason's parents' house for a barbecue and some beers. I haven't seen any of them since the trip to Winter Park. We show up with a package of bratwursts and a six-pack.

I sit down in a lawn chair and start chatting with Jason's dad—probably about the weather or football or some similar topic. Jason comes ripping out of the house, down the stairs, around the patio, and then stops in front of my chair. I watch him trying to place my face, trying to recall exactly who I am. He knows me, but it takes him just a second to mark me.

"Hey, Jason," I say. "How's it going?"

"Hi," he says, stopping just to stare at me a bit more. "You're the one who gave me brain damage."

He points at me and rubs his hand on the back of his head. He makes a sour face, then turns around and runs back into the house. His dad apologizes, but I tell him not to worry about it. It's not a big deal. Really, it's not. I'm over it. But we both know this isn't true.

It's times like these that make me think I'll never escape my own body.

Horse, Smallest.

The smallest breed of horse is the Falabella, bred by Julio Falabella [who also owned the tallest horse, "Firpon" at 7 feet 1 inch and 2,976 lbs.], developed over a period of 45 years by crossing and recrossing a small group of undersized English thoroughbreds with Shetland ponies. Adult specimens range from 15 inches to 30 inches at the shoulder and weigh from 40 to 80 lbs. Foals standing 3 hands (12 inches) have been recorded twice by Norman J. Mitchell of Glenorie, New South Wales, Australia in the cases of "Tung Dynasty" (February 8, 1978) and "Quicksilver" (1975).

The upper accepted limit for the American Miniature Horse Breeders Association is 34 inches. (1980, 76)

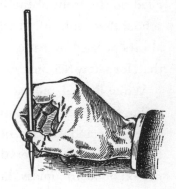

Transportation, Most Dangerous.

After Matt died in his car, I knew I needed to make efforts to get out of Kansas, away from home. Lawrence was just saturated with memory, and I felt bloated with grief. So one summer Rachel and I spent three weeks traveling by bus in Costa Rica. We'd always liked getting away in the summers, and I suppose I was hoping for some kind of diversion, some freedom from my own body, but I never felt so giant, so misfit, as when I was riding those ancient, creaking sardine cans that pass for public transportation.

There was no physical way for me to fit in the plastic seats. Built for people half my size, they were simply too close together. So I usually stood packed in the aisle, sweating with the others. I would occasionally recall the thick black letters stenciled on the front of the bus Matt and I rode to elementary school that said, NO STANDEES PERMITTED, and while I've always puzzled over the word *standee*, it seemed pretty clear that, for safety reasons, you shouldn't be standing in the aisles.

While Rachel and the locals fit just fine in the buses, the ceilings were too low for me even to stand upright, so I had to slump or stand with my head cocked to the side, giving me a disorienting view of everything. I was almost always the tallest person onboard, unless there happened to be another American tourist or two.

One trip we took up from the coast, I stood in the aisle of

this ancient Volvo bus, putting my life into the hands of the driver as we crossed rivers on bridges consisting of nothing more than a couple of planks. After we had survived a climb up the infamous, twisting Cerro de los Muertes (Hill of the Dead) without tumbling off the edge and dying in a horrible twist of steel and flesh and jungle foliage, it seemed appropriate that a woman would vomit in the bus just three minutes before her stop.

Her fluids sloshed up and down the aisle, splashing on my boots, and I just tried to breathe through my mouth while chunks of corn and pepper floated around in a thin soup of stomach bile. I closed my eyes and imagined myself flying down a mountain trail on my motorcycle, following Matt and Dad, the scent of pine stinging my sinuses. At my lowest moments I even longed for the comforts of Kansas and wanted to click my heels and send us back from this Land of the Swarthy Munchkins, but my boots were covered in puke and I was caged up in that vomitorium on wheels.

• • •

During our travels in Costa Rica and other places, when I'd tell people we're from Kansas, they often thought I grew up slopping hogs and graduated high school with thirteen other kids I'd known since we were all born in the same barn. They had a Hollywood image of Kansas in their heads. But the truth is I probably saw more drugs, sex, and violence growing up and going to school in Lawrence than most will see in a lifetime.

One of my best friends for years was a homosexual junkie who, in his early thirties, worked in the bakery at the grocery store where I was a bagger and checker. I think Henry liked the idea of having me around, and I liked hanging out with him. He was a nice guy, pretty smart, and he didn't make me feel strange. He always just liked me for who I was. I didn't have to pretend with Henry, didn't have to try to be cool. Visiting his house was always an escape from my own world, always bizarre and endlessly fascinating.

I have clear memories of sitting on the floor in his bedroom reading a book while the five other people in the room passed around a silver tray lined out with cocaine and huffed white powder up their noses through a rolled-up ten-dollar bill. A skinny girl offered me the tray, but Henry reached out and took it before I could even set my book down.

"He doesn't do blow," he said.

"That's cool," she said and sort of giggled. She wore a mini-skirt and knee-high black boots. She sat cross-legged on the floor, and anyone in the room could see the blue polka dots on her panties. She wasn't like any of the girls I knew.

Henry wouldn't let me do cocaine or anything more serious than pain pills or Valium—the ones he'd slip to me occasionally with the vague promise "You'll like it." But I wasn't that interested in cocaine to begin with. It didn't seem like my kind of drug. I had enough sweat and anxiety without it.

Henry's room was like *The Golden Girls* meets *Trainspotting*. The walls were covered with collectible plates, glass animals, and porcelain figurines—the kind of stuff my grandmother kept in lighted display cases. The floors were covered with cigarette wrappers, magazines, fast-food packaging, ashtrays, and dirt piled on top of dirt. You could lose something in there and not find it for days or weeks or even months.

Henry had already planned his funeral and had songs picked out for the playlist along with designated pallbearers and performers. He talked often about his own death and, depending on the week, already had one foot in the grave. Part of his plan consisted of doling out his prized possessions to close friends, and I have to admit feeling somewhat honored when he pulled the Wizard of Oz plate—the one with Dorothy, Toto, the Tin Man, the Scarecrow, and the Lion all dancing down the Yellow Brick Road—off the wall and promised it to me. He peeled off a strip of masking tape, pressed it onto the back of the plate, and wrote my name in big, black letters.

"When I die, it's yours," he said and hung the plate back on the wall.

I asked him about the other plates, and Henry ticked off the names of the people he had promised them to. Every single one was destined for a boy I knew.

"You're special," he said as he pulled a long drag from his cigarette. "You know that, right."

"What do you mean?"

"I mean you're better than this," he said, sort of gesturing around the room with his cigarette.

"You can get out of here. You can go places." He paused to take another drag. "I watched you play basketball on TV the other night, and I saw that interview with your shirt off," he said and kind of giggled. "You did good. You sound smart."

"Thanks, man," I said. "That's nice to hear."

"Well, don't get all sentimental on me now. I was just hoping you'd let me suck you off," he said and laughed, his cigarette bouncing vigorously in his lips.

I knew that he was only half joking about sucking me off

and that he was mostly sincere about the other stuff he said. Henry was one of the first friends with whom I could be completely honest, and somehow, when Henry said I was OK, I knew he was right. I knew, no matter how lost I might have felt at times, there was always a way out. I could always rebound. Somehow it sunk in more when Henry said it than when parents or teachers or anyone else did.

Henry messed up with a needle once, got an air bubble trapped in his vein, and went into cardiac arrest in the middle of a Sunday brunch buffet. I wasn't there, but I heard about it later. His hand swelled up like a sausage and sent a bubble to his heart. Henry lived, but this was around the same time another friend overdosed on coke and tumbled down a flight of stairs, separating his shoulder and winding up in a hospital bed charged with numerous counts of drug possession.

All at once it seemed fate had conspired to convince me that I didn't really need to mess with cocaine or any other white drugs. I saw too many friends collapsing in on themselves, imploding before my eyes. I had lived a life of risk, but this was one time when my finely honed sense of fear worked to my advantage and convinced me there were other ways to have fun, other ways to escape.

• • •

When I moved into my lake cabin on the outskirts of Lawrence, I needed an escape. The cabin was part of an old private hunting and fishing club that had been around since the late 1800s, and it was distinguished by a giant lodge building erected in 1912 and surrounded by stately cottonwood trees. I loved living there. It was good to be away from town, to have the woods and the water nearby. It was easy to disappear. It was the kind of place I needed to heal and rebuild and grow new skin.

Shortly after I moved in, my best friend, Rob, got the job of caretaker for the club grounds. He lived in a mobile home trailer that jutted out from the back of the lodge like a hairless aluminum tail. Basically his job consisted of mowing a shitload of grass and walking around with a big flashlight, rattling locks and peeking in windows.

Rob and I often spent our Friday nights fishing for channel catfish, largemouth bass, and crappie. He was a brother to me in those years after Matt died—still is—and we'd often spend hours sitting in lawn chairs, telling stories, or just staring at the moonlight on the water and listening to the trains pass, or the rumble of the coal-fired power plant in the distance.

We'd camp on the banks of this oxbow lake and sit up all night tossing chunks of raw chicken liver out into the water, waiting for the telltale tugging of a catfish bite. Most times the little bites were bullheads, tiny shit fish that inevitably swallowed the hook, so you waited and waited and waited for the big ones. It was a meditative, Zen sort of experience that more young men should probably have.

It can take a while to catch a fish. Sometimes when it was dark we'd hang bells from the tips of our poles and listen for the ringing of a bite, and more than once I got so excited I jerked the pole to set the hook and sent the bell flying off into the trees. We had a lot of fun, and we weren't out driving around drunk, rolling cars, overdosing, and getting arrested.

The worst that could happen to us was maybe falling in the water, but we'd spent enough time in the lake to know that most of it's shallow enough to stand in. The lake had its share of mystery and danger. It was just a different kind, the kind that lurks beneath muddy brown water and surfaces only occasionally. We were never afraid of being pulled under. It was more a fear of what might come up to the surface. In Kansas a lot of people dump their secrets in lakes and ponds. People just disappear in the Kaw River, and for a while it seemed like a dead Indian was surfacing every few months.

We didn't worry too much about that sort of thing, but we had active enough imaginations to wonder what swam below us. We'd heard stories about catfish in the Kaw the size of a Volkswagen Beetle, and we knew this lake had once been part of the river. Still, the biggest thing we'd ever caught there was a twelve-pound flathead catfish that put up one hell of a fight. That fish was almost as big around as it was long and a deep brown, almost black color; but still nothing compared with the thing I hooked into one day with Rob.

A largemouth bass or a crappie will jump out of the water when it's hooked, or at least come close and give you a peek. But this fish took my lure and dove straight to the bottom. That's what a catfish or carp will do—play with you down there, wrap you around a tree stump or a rock, and snap your line. They're tricksters, fighters. I tried to reel in the fish, but he pulled the canoe around as if our weight was nothing at all, like a big dog walking its owner. Afraid to lose it before we'd even seen it, Rob and I paddled to the bank and beached the canoe.

Neither of us spoke. We knew this sort of thing didn't happen all the time. We knew this was different. I stepped out of the boat, played with the drag, and began to crank the reel as I backed up the boat ramp. The spool whined from the strain. I let the fish run for a while before I reeled hard again. Rob crouched down at the edge of the water, and I pulled. My pole almost doubled over, and I hoped the eight-pound test would hold. I pulled and pulled, and something appeared slowly from the green water, rolling and flashing beneath the surface, an ungodly thing—a great, scaly carp that must have weighed thirty or forty pounds.

Colored the sickly pallid white of a corpse, the fish looked as if he had never left the lake bottom, never seen sunlight until that moment. Rob grabbed the line and yanked the body up onto the bank. I watched him there, down by the water, and I was glad he was with the fish instead of me. He's better at these things than I am.

I moved closer, still a little afraid of what I had dragged up from below. The carp's bulging lips gasped as the short, rubbery, white spines quivered around the edges of its mouth. Scales, each the size of a quarter, heaved and spread with every breath. Neither of us wanted to touch it. We just toed it with our shoes. The fish flopped on the sand, a beastly, humped thing, its black, pearly eyes wide and shiny, my Mepps number 2 Bucktail stuck unexplainably in its dorsal fin. The body made a dull *thwop* noise every time it hit the sand. I handed Rob my pocketknife. He cut the line and pushed the thing back under the surface, where it belonged.

• • •

As much as I love spending time in lakes and rivers, I'm not a big fan of the ocean experience. Agreeing to travel to Costa Rica was a big step for me. I have trouble with the idea that

211

I'm floating above large animals that could possibly eat me. Plus, I don't like the powerlessness I feel when I'm in the ocean.

I know it sounds strange, but I feel as if I'm climbing into a living, breathing beast that just wants to churn me up and spit me out with the flotsam. The first week we were in the country a group of German tourists celebrating a World Cup victory in soccer were just standing around in the ocean laughing, cheering, having a good time, when a wave came up, slammed into them, and sucked five of them out to sea. They all died.

Rachel was kind and patient with me and didn't demand that we go snorkeling or scuba diving immediately. One of the first things we did was go horseback riding on the beach with a local guide named Enrique, who appeared to be about twelve years old, skinny as a rail, but had a wise look in his eyes. He wore a battered straw hat, faded gym shorts, and he rode bareback in the surf.

Aside from a motorcycle or a bicycle, horseback has to be the purest form of *private* transportation. You're actually riding another mammal. No sharing seats. No ceilings. No traffic. No vomit on your boots. I see why cowboys like them so much. It's a partnership, a friendship even.

The poor, bony horse they gave me looked like it barely outweighed me. I took one look at him and knew we'd never be friends. When I was mounted in the saddle, my feet nearly dangled in the surf. I felt like the World's Largest Horseback Tourist. Enrique bounced along in the surf and laughed at the spectacle of my miniature stallion and me.

If that wasn't enough to make me feel like I could never be a free-ranging cowboy, just last year we went riding in the mountains with friends. When we pulled up, there was a small sign posted next to the stable's cashier that read, "Weight Limit 250 lbs." I listed mine at a dishonest 230, and the guides gave me the biggest horse in the barn, a Percheron-mix draft horse named Froggle, who was bred to pull massive sleighs through six-foot drifts of snow. He reminded me of pictures I've seen in the Guinness Books of giant horses like Firpon with hoofs the size of beer kegs. Everyone else had these svelte little mares and muscled stallions. Froggle looked like a goddamn Clydesdale. I sat up higher than all the others and looked down on their puny, normal-size horses. I didn't know whether to feel honored or humiliated.

Motionlessness. **The longest that any person has voluntarily remained motionless is 6 hours 31 minutes by William Fuqua at Dillard's Department Store, Fort Worth, Texas on July 22, 1978.**

Staff Sgt. Samuel B. Moody, U.S.A.F., was punished by being forced to stand at attention for 53 hours in Narumi prison camp, Nagoya, Japan, in the spring of 1945. He survived to write *Reprieve from Hell*. (1980, 51)

Living Statue. **William Fuqua (right) required the services of a bodyguard in his 1978 record attempt. In a 1975 personal appearance he was stabbed in the back by a man who could not believe that he was real. (1980, 51)**

Airplanes are positively torturous for me. I'd rather lie on a bed of nails than spend time in those things. I have mild claustrophobia, but it's really more of an overactive self-consciousness,

213

similar to what I experience in crowded bars or parties or public restrooms. I feel misfit for the space I occupy, oversize for
my environment, and generally oafish.

Buses are bad, but nothing gets me cranked up like airplanes. Now that I have a son, I worry more about crashing
than I ever have before. I worry that Malcolm won't get a
chance to live. But what really bothers me—what have always
bothered me—are the seats. They make me feel imprisoned
and powerless, like a big, grumpy bear caught in a trap. I'm
surrounded by people *and* I'm restrained. I couldn't feel more
incapable, more at odds with myself; and I haven't even mentioned what it is like to wrestle an overactive toddler for the duration of a flight.

It's the holidays. It's always the holidays when we fly, and
Rachel and I are taking Malcolm back to Kansas for Thanks-
giving. We spent last night in a motel near the airport and
woke up at 5:00 A.M. to catch a shuttle van to the terminal.
The flight is packed and delayed by a half hour or more. By
the time we're done, it will have taken us all day to get to
Lawrence, and just the thought of it already makes me nause-
ated.

Rachel will listen to me say several times how we could
have *driven* home in the same amount of time. The air in the
plane is thick with human stink and pierced occasionally by
Malcolm's chirps and squeals as he rolls and tumbles around
on our laps. There are no buffer zones between me and Rachel, just a plastic armrest, so I end up leaning into her much
of the time.

My surgically repaired knee presses against the seat in front
of me. Soon it will stiffen and the pain will shoot up my leg,

into my back. My shoulders are too wide to fit in the seat, so I have to fold them inward. If I drop the tray table, I am immobilized—my forearms, hands, and head the only things that can wiggle freely.

Because he's still young enough, we carry Malcolm on our laps. He has just started talking and likes to say "Hi. How are you?" to strangers, but when they respond "I'm good. How are you?" he says, "No," and shakes his head. He does this to the woman sitting next to Rachel. Several times. Then he announces to the passengers, "I have a big poop, Daddy," when he doesn't at all. It's all quite amusing. Rachel and I laugh nervously. *Isn't he funny?*

It's hard enough for me to be in an airplane, but now I have this small mammal crawling around on top of me. He stomps on my crotch and reaches over the seat in front to grab at an old lady's hair. I pull his hand back and remind him that "we don't touch."

"I think this is the last time he can fly without his own seat," Rachel says as she reaches for the bribery bag of M&M's.

"Yeah," I say as he honks my nose. "I think you're right."

Malcolm is getting big—too big to pass for his age sometimes, too big for our laps—and I see so much of myself in his body. The thick torso, the long arms, the stout legs and big satellite ears. I'm overly conscious about calling him "big boy" and find myself cringing when strangers comment on his size.

I want my son to feel like he fits in the world, even if he doesn't.

We're sitting there, just waiting for a few passengers, trying to wrangle Malcolm, when this very stylish man rushes down the aisle and sits in the seat immediately in front of me. He wears a sheer brown polyester shirt that shows his nipples, and his curly, black hair has a thick, oily sheen. He's talking on a cell phone the whole way down the aisle, reporting his every movement in great detail.

"I'm boarding now."

Pause.

"Yes, now."

Pause.

"It was delayed."

Pause.

"Right now. I'm sitting down right now."

Pause.

"Yes, now."

Pause.

"Okay. Bye."

Malcolm of course is climbing around, chattering away, and trying to grab the guy's shiny hair. And before we even roll out of the gate, Mr. Fancy Nipple flags down the stewardess and asks if he can switch seats. He doesn't even bother to look and see that the plane is completely full, doesn't even consider that he's kept me here—all of us here—for hours it seemed while he's talking with his dog sitter or his stylist or his accountant on the phone. I think he's afraid Malcolm might mess up his hair. We're barely off the ground before he orders a tiny bottle of wine and pulls a glossy fashion magazine out from his leather satchel.

When we finally get in the air, Malcolm curls up on Rachel's lap and falls asleep. The flight from Denver to Kansas City is so short that there's maybe a ten-minute window when the "Fasten Seat Belts" sign isn't glowing orange and mocking me. I try to read something from the in-flight magazine, but the shiny glow of the guy's hair distracts me, and next thing I know, he lays his seat back and locks me into a restraint better suited for Hannibal Lecter.

The captain's muffled voice comes over the intercom, and I think he says something about Omaha or Wichita. I can't be sure. The orange light goes off with a *ping*, but I'm belted into a straitjacket, not allowed to "move freely about the cabin," and once again reminded of my incapacitation, my powerlessness. I flail my arms wildly and feel like screaming at the top of my lungs.

Deep breaths. Count to ten. Relax.

It will all be over soon.

I feel like a statistical anomaly, an oddity seat designers couldn't factor into their decisions. So I turn again to the Guinness Books. I pull my tattered yellow copy of the Giant 1980 Super-Edition out of the seat pocket and disappear into a refuge of print and paper while the stewardess blocks my exit with the drink cart. I turn to my Guinness friends. I turn to stories, hoping the right kind will set me free.

Typing, Longest.

Mrs. Marva Drew, 51, of Waterloo, Iowa, between 1968 and November 30, 1974, typed the numbers 1 to 1,000,000 (in words) on a manual typewriter. She used 2,473 pages. When asked why, she replied, "But I love to type." (1980, 487)

Escape, Greatest.

In the picture, Marva Drew sits with her arms crossed and propped on a stack of white paper. In the foreground the type-writer, black and polished, has been turned slightly to face the camera. Three sheets of paper fan out on the table like a tennis skirt and seem to reach out of the picture space.

Marva's hair is curled into a tight helmet, and her forehead shines like white porcelain. There is a lot of white. But behind her the room is dark. The sharp lines of her horn-rimmed glasses cut across her face and hide her eyes. Her smile is un-mistakable—this full-mouthed, overbite smile. She is so full of pride, so happy to be in The *Guinness Book of World Records*. She looks supremely satisfied.

Of course I can't help but wonder about the gaps, the room where she sits and types, the house she haunts with her habit. I hear the constant drumming of keys punctuated with the intermittent thump of the space bar and the rewarding *ping* of the carriage bell. Who listens to this? Who loves this? I see Marva secluded in a basement bathroom. She might use the toilet for a chair and sit behind a card table, several reams of paper stacked in the shower. Her husband has prob-ably covered the ceiling and door with soundproof tiles. He just ignores her. Her kids probably think she's crazy. But I think she's wonderful.

Typing, Slowest. **Chinese typewriters are so complex that even the most skilled operator cannot select characters from the 1,500 offered at a rate of more than 11 words a minute. The Hoang typewriter produced in 1962 now has 5,850 Chinese characters. The keyboard is 2 feet wide and 17 inches high. (1980, 487)**

I see Marva Drew in the morning before she goes to work, and part of me envies her escape. I see her sitting in her bathrobe, thumping on the keys for thirty minutes. At night when she returns from her job, Marva disappears again into the bathroom and won't emerge until the children are pounding on the door, begging for dinner. She does this for six years.

I suspect that Marva is self-medicating. There's something soothing in the rhythmic clicking of the typewriter, the violent smack of the carriage return. Marva doesn't care for words. There is no love for language motivating her. She's not a writer. She types (or spells) numbers. "One. Two. Three. Four." She pounds out counting patterns. It's like exercise. "One hundred one, one hundred two, one hundred three." There must be something meditative about the chatter of letter keys, like the comforting cradle of a rocking chair or the numbing effects of a metronome. I wonder if she reads books or magazines while she types. I wonder what she thinks about, if she thinks about anything at all, or if it's just an hour or two hours of nothingness she needs to survive.

I have to believe there's some splintered plane in her life, a landscape of loss she sands down and smoothes over with the repeated pounding of the keys. I don't know for sure, but I suspect she channels her family's compulsions—as if she's plugged into their psyches. She kills time, typing away the worry, while her husband takes her fragile sons out to shoot guns and ride motorcycles and drink from pony bottles of Miller beer. Maybe she never even goes to work. She's just tuned in to the pulse of her family. She's the World's Most Patient Mother, World's Greatest Typist, World's Greatest Ghost of the Basement. I can see all of this so clearly. Marva has a son who loves her unconditionally, a large boy with an overactive imagination and a fresh swath of scar tissue. I can see the connections. But nothing I can imagine comes close to touching what typing truly means to Marva Drew. Nothing I can imagine really explains her presence in the Guinness Books. That's part of the reason I like her so much.

Acknowledgments, Most Deserving Of.

World-Record-size thanks:

To my family and my parents (all of them) for your undying love and support. To Mom and Dad for telling me stories and teaching me more than I could ever imagine. To my brothers, Matt and Cory, for being the best any man could ask for. To all my extended family and Rachel's family for your stories, your personalities, and (after this book) your patience.

To good friends past and present, including Rob Shufelt, Ronnie Buhr, Matt Cobb, Joe Triplett, Jeremy Friedman, Scott Patton, Jeff Brown, Dale Hazlett, Megan Arnaud, Darrel Brannock, Kristy Eumont, Sarah Randolph, Danielle Akua Smith, Jenny Wortman, Justin Hocking, Jill Darling, Tom Bissell, and many, many others.

To all my friends and co-workers at Colorado State University—especially Marcy Christensen, Blane Harding, Ann Gill, Gaye DiGregorio, Madlyn D'Andrea, Shari Hattam, Linda Stoddard, Kerry Nakasone, Stephanie G'Schwind, and everyone else at CASA and the Dean's Office.

To all my teachers: Russ Shafer-Landau, Jim Carothers, and Tom Lorenz at the University of Kansas; and everyone in the English department at Colorado State University—but most especially Steven Schwartz, John Calderazzo, Leslee Becker, and Deanna Ludwin.

To my writing group, The Minions (Matt Roberts, Sophie

Moore, Todd Mitchell, Oz Spies, Emily Wortman-Wunder, Jeff Faas, Kerri Mitchell, and Jamie Kembrey), for all your energy and influence. Thanks especially to Matt Roberts for being a true friend, critic, amazing writer, fellow father, and for always making me laugh.

To the Colorado Council for the Arts and Bread Loaf Writers' Conference for support and opportunity.

To all the magazines that published my work (*Fourth Genre, Post Road, Puerto del Sol, Quarterly West, River Teeth, Quarter After Eight, Salt Hill*); thanks also to *Many Mountains Moving* and the *Colorado Review* for letting me hang around.

To the McWhirter twins, the Guinness World Records organization, and all the Guinness World Record Holders for their dreams, obsessions, and accidents. Specifically I want to thank Benny and Billy McCrary, Shridhar Chillal, Marva Drew, and Jay Gwaltney.

To my agent, Doug Stewart, for hard work, direction, and support. To my editor, Denise Roy, for faith, vision, wisdom, and to David Rosenthal for just taking a chance on me in the first place.

Finally and most importantly I want to thank my beautiful and brilliant wife, Rachel—best friend, best reader, best everything—and my world-shaking son, Malcolm. It's all for you.

— SWC

Grateful acknowledgments to the following for permission to use previously published work:

Soft Skull Press: Justin Hocking et al., eds., *Life and Limb: Skateboarders Write from the Deep End* (New York: Soft Skull Press, 2004). For an earlier version of the chapter "Diet, Strangest."

River Teeth, A Journal of Nonfiction Narrative; Quarterly West; Puerto del Sol; and *Post Road Magazine.* For parts of this book originally published in different forms with different titles in those magazines. Parts of my book were also published as a portion of my MFA thesis at Colorado State University, 2002.